ATTACKS
IN
AIKIDO

ATTACKS
IN
AIKIDO
How to do Kogeki, the Attack Techniques

STEFAN STENUDD

arriba.se

Stefan Stenudd is a 6 dan Aikikai Swedish aikido instructor, Vice Chairman of the International Aikido Federation, member of the Swedish Aikikai Grading Committee, and President of the Swedish Budo & Martial Arts Federation. He is also an author, artist, and historian of ideas. He has published a number of books in Swedish and English, both fiction and non-fiction. Among the latter is a Swedish interpretation of the Chinese classic *Tao Te Ching*, and of the Japanese samurai classic *Book of Five Rings* by Miyamoto Musashi. His novels explore existential subjects from stoneage drama to science fiction, but lately stay more and more focused on the present. He has also written some plays for the stage and the screen. In the history of ideas he studies the thought patterns of creation myths, as well as Aristotle's *Poetics*. He has his own extensive website, which contains a lot of aikido material, among other things:
> **www.stenudd.com**

Also by Stefan Stenudd:
Aikido Principles, 2008.
Aikibatto: Sword Exercises for Aikido Students, 2007, 2009.
Qi: Increase your Life Energy, 2008.
Life Energy Encyclopedia, 2008.
Cosmos of the Ancients, 2007.
Your Health and Your Horoscope, 2009.
All's End, 2007.
Murder, 2006.

Second edition.

Attacks in Aikido: How to do Kogeki, the Attack Techniques
Copyright © Stefan Stenudd 2008, 2009.
Book design by the author.
All rights reserved.
ISBN: 978-91-7894-025-7
Publisher: Arriba, Malmö Sweden.
www.arriba.se

Contents

Katadori menuchi, shoulder grip and head strike. The hand side strike is a symbol for the shomen sword attack.

Foreword

Aikido is full of paradoxes. It is a peaceful martial art, which is in itself a seemingly impossible contradiction. But the principles and solutions of aikido actually make it true. Another paradox is that aikido really consists solely of defense techniques, but it is essential to learn attacks in order to master that defense.

Of course, the attacker is always the loser in aikido practice. We take turns attacking, so that our training partners can exercise the defenses. The goal of the training, though, is the defense. Learning how to attack is only sort of a side-effect.

Nonetheless, if you want to increase your skills in the aikido defense techniques, you must also improve your attack technique skills accordingly. They depend on one another. It is by experiencing advanced attacks that you are able to develop an advanced defense.

And when you have reached a fundamental understanding of attacks and the principles behind them, you will find the way to an aikido that transforms the attacker-defender polarity into a flow of forces, a dance of sorts, where the pair is so united that it seems like a solo. That's when aikido becomes really enchanting.

There are many books about aikido, but as far as I know this is the first one about the attack techniques used in aikido practice. It is intended to work as a manual for beginners, as well as a useful tool for the advanced students.

As for my understanding of attacks in aikido, I am in debt to several prominent aikido teachers. Three come immediately to mind: Toshikazu Ichimura, who was my first Japanese teacher, always insisted on full-powered and focused attacks, Shoji Nishio was a master of precision in everything, with vast experience gathered from many *budo* arts, and Nobuyoshi Tamura creates a *koan* riddle each time he grabs my wrist.

I am also grateful to my dojo members Tomas Ohlsson and Jonas Dahlqvist, who assisted in the photo sessions, and to training partners as well as photographers at my seminars in Sweden, the Czech Republic, and Germany.

Malmö, August 2008
Stefan Stenudd

Taninzugake, defense against several attackers, at a seminar in Pardubice, Czech Republic. Photo by Leos Matousek.

Introduction

In aikido training, the actual aikido technique is always a defense, and not an attack. It is usually trained in a paired exercise, where one uses aikido techniques to defend against the other's attacks. So, an attack in aikido is merely a service to the defender, so that he or she can practice the aikido techniques.

Therefore, it is quite common in aikido that both training partners focus almost completely on the defender role, and neglect that of the attacker. It can go so far as to a state very near sleep when attacking, as if this is a moment for rest, until again it is time to be the defender.

Such a way of training is unfortunate in so many ways. Mainly, it causes one's focus soon to become blurred also in the defender role. Without working on increasingly advanced attacks, it is impossible to advance in one's aikido. We need to be more skilled as attackers, to be able to teach each other higher skills in the defense.

I do not primarily mean the self-defense aspect, although that also needs to be considered. Here I think of the way (*do*) of aikido. When attacks get more precise, focused, and sophisticated, then they stimulate the refinement of your aikido and your understanding of its nature. When you show just as much care about your attacks as you do about your defense, then it will truly be aikido.

It's more fun, too, if you devote yourself to the attacker's mind and strategy, when your partner is the defender – and then switch to the defender mind when it's your turn to do aikido techniques. The shift of behavior is good mental training, indeed. Sort of instant acting: to switch immediately from one role to its opposite. You'll have twice the fun at practice.

Tori and uke

The defender in aikido is called *tori*. It literally means to take, fetch, catch, hold, seize, pick up, and such. Its pictogram (*kanji*) consists of two signs: the one for the ear, and the one for 'again' or 'on the other hand'. So, the combination suggests attentiveness, and correction of some sort. The second sign also suggests a hand, thereby making the combination mean grabbing someone by the ear, like parents do when correcting or disciplining their children.

The attacker is called *uke*, which means to receive, accept, undergo, and so forth. It is used for catching a ball, answering the phone, or undergoing an operation, among many other things. This kanji consists of three parts. On top is the sign for a claw or nail, below that the sign for a lid, and at the bottom the sign of 'again' or the hand (the same as in tori). This implies passing something from one hand to another, where the upper one is the stronger and the lower weaker – both because of the signs used and their positions.

So, the words used for the defender and the attacker of aikido suggest that the former is the teacher and the latter the student. The exercise between them seems to be of the nature that the defender is teaching something to the attacker.

Aikido

Ryotedori, gripping both wrists, at a children's class in Stockholm. Photo by Gunilla Welin.

Of course, this can be understood as aikido showing attackers the folly of their way. If you attack, you are defeated, so you should learn never to do so. I remember that Shoji Nishio, a very prominent aikido teacher, stressed this repeatedly in his classes. Tori's task is to show uke the futility of attacking. Therefore, the aikido techniques should be compassionate and never harmful. Otherwise, how would the attacker be able to benefit from the experience?

The terms used also suggest, although indirectly, who is the winner and who the loser. There is no competition in aikido, therefore neither winner nor loser. Uke should not be defeated. Instead, the attack should be used as a possibility to demonstrate the principles of aikido, the martial art moving away from battle up to the point of making it non-existent. The defender is the teacher correcting the attacker, who is the student, by transforming the attack into something that is to the delight of both.

For the purpose of this book, it is important to observe how the choice of terms for the defender and the attacker point out the necessity for the latter to expect a learning experience. We practice the role of the defender in order to

Miyamoto Musashi fights Tsukahara Bokuden. Woodprint by Yoshitoshi, 1885.

learn aikido, but the true purpose of aikido is to teach the attacker. So, the role of the attacker cannot be ignored.

The legendary 17th century samurai Miyamoto Musashi said that the teacher is the needle, and the student is the thread. Again an example of one leading, and the other being led. And again it stresses the importance of the uke role as that of the real student. When the garment is completed, the thread remains in it, continuing to fulfill its function, whereas the needle is long gone.

So, let's treat the uke role with the sincerity that it demands. Let's learn proper attacks and the true mind of the attacker.

In aikido, other words are sometimes used for the defender – such as *nage*, simply meaning the one who throws, or *shite*, the leading hand, the protagonist, or the hero (like in a play). That is a pity, since they don't hold the same symbolic meanings as the word tori does – especially in relation to the word uke. Another word than uke is rarely used for the attacker in aikido.

Kogeki 攻撃

Below, I present all the basic attack techniques (*kogeki* or *kogekiho*) in aikido, and explain what to think about when training them. I don't try to be complete. For example, some difficult kicks and some rare and odd grips are missing, as well as some armed attacks. What is included, though, covers most of what is trained in any aikido dojo.

Some of these attacks are very commonly used in aikido practice, such as wrist grips (*katatedori*), fist strikes (*tsuki*), and open hand strikes (*shomenuchi* and *yokomenuchi*). Others are rare, in some cases barely practiced at all, for example the bear hug (*kakaedori*), the sleeve grip (*sodedori*), or grabbing both the shoulder and the wrist (*kata katatedori*).

It would be a pity if some exotic attack forms disappeared completely from the aikido curriculum. Each attack has its own lesson to give, and shows different aspects of the aikido techniques when used against it. If practice is limited to just a few attacks, then the techniques are not learned properly, and not examined at enough depth.

The basic idea in aikido regarding the inclusion or exclusion of attack forms is simply that every possible attack should be included. Contrary to many other martial arts, in aikido we try to familiarize ourselves with whatever attack makes any sense to an attacker. The aikido techniques should be applicable to just about any situation, so they need to be tried against as many different attack types as possible. In most other martial arts, the techniques are trained against a selection of attacks only.

This broad spectrum of attacks in aikido makes it next to impossible to master them all. Some seem easy enough, but even something as basic as grabbing a wrist can be done with more or less skill. The more the skill, the better for the purpose of learning how to defend against the attacks with aikido techniques.

This may seem like an impossible task, but there are some general principles that apply to all kinds of attacks. If these basics are trained, you will quickly notice that you in-

Gyakuhanmi katatedori, wrist grip, on a seminar at Enighet, the author's dojo in Malmö, Sweden. Photo by Anders Heinonen.

crease your skills also with things that you do not practice that often. The basics of attacking are presented and explained in one chapter of this book. I advice you to read it before you go on to the presentations of the actual attack forms.

Tables of techniques
This book contains tables of the aikido techniques, combined with the basic attack forms. The tables indicate the level of difficulty for each combination of attack form and aikido technique. There are also some comprised explanations and pointers.

In the tables, I have tried to be as complete as is reasonable, including all the basic combinations – and a lot of not so basic ones.

Aikido is a vast system of techniques. The basic pinnings and throws are not that many, but several of them have both an *omote* and an *ura* form, often differing substantially. Also, each technique is slightly modified depending on what attack it is used against. So, the aikido curriculum ends up consisting of a few thousand more or less different techniques.

I have included the tables to show this complexity, and also to arrange it somewhat systematically. I hope that it is of some use to aikido practitioners.

Glossary

The book ends with a dictionary of aikido terminology, where the Japanese terms used in aikido are listed and explained shortly. Some of the terms are from other martial arts, but have a certain relevance also for aikido practitioners.

This is the same glossary as the one already published in my book *Aikido: The Peaceful Martial Art*. I included it here too, for the convenience of the reader.

The terminology of aikido is not an exact science. Some names are not used the same way in different aikido styles. Mostly in this glossary, when relevant, I present the meaning applied by the Hombu Dojo of Aikikai.

Another inconsistency is the transcription of the terms, i.e. how they are spelled with western letters. The spelling commonly used in aikido is in many cases different from the one used by linguists and Japanologists. This is true already for the word aikido, which should actually be spelled *aikidou* or *aikidô*.

These anomalies of the aikido terminology stem from its emergence through aikido practice in many different parts of the world, where the terms were transcribed sort of sluggishly, with little consideration of linguistics. Already at the Hombu Dojo, the aikido terms were initially treated without much systematic concern.

Maybe this will change in the future, if some standard is produced and established internationally – at least for English transcription, and hopefully for what techniques should have what names. Certainly, there are inconsistencies with the terminology for the attack forms as well. In this book, though, I have tried to use the most widely accepted and accurate terms. When this has not been possible, I mention it in the comments about the techniques. The glossary, too, contains alternative terms where such are widely used.

Taaisabaki evasion from maegeri, front kick, at a seminar in Pardubice, Czech Republic. Photo by Leos Matousek.

Aikido

Attack basics

The most important thing for uke to remember when attacking tori during aikido practice, is to be sincere. Commit yourself to the attack, as if intending to succeed with it. Focus on it, each time it is repeated. Pursue it, so that your aim on tori remains. Learn to do the attack form skillfully, and strive to increase that skill as you continue with your aikido practice.

In short, regard the attacks with the same sincerity as if they were martial arts of their own. In a way they are, since many attack forms are actually loans from other Japanese martial arts, such as jujitsu, karatedo, or kendo.

This does not mean that you should compete with tori, by making it as difficult as you can for him or her to execute the aikido technique. It's not a contest, but a learning situation, where both participants cooperate for their mutual progress.

Empty mind

Be distinct and focused in your attacks, but not overly aggressive. And each time you attack anew, you should act as if it is the first time, as if you have no idea of what the response will be.

Of course an aikido technique can be blocked and countered when you know beforehand which one it is. That has little meaning in practice. Instead, make your attacks neutral in the way that they do not presuppose anything. Forget what happened the last time.

That is not easy when you practice the same technique with your partner for a long time, but the exercise of pretending not to be aware of tori's response is a very rewarding one. It actually improves your ability both to attack and to defend yourself, since you keep your mind open and your body in an overall ready position.

Essentially, it is kind of an 'empty mind' exercise. You charge without preconceptions, and you remain in this men-

Suwarikokyuho with Nobuyoshi Tamura, 8 dan Aikikai, and the author. Photo by Anders Heinonen.

tal state all through the aikido technique. You are in the moment, not what preceded it, nor do you give any thought to what comes next. When you attack, you open your mind to *takemusu*, martial art born in the moment, and allow for tori to treat it in an *aiki* manner. Your body will respond naturally if not blocked by your mind. Just remain in your attacker spirit, and experience how aikido transforms the situation.

It is quite joyous.

Pursue

It is necessary that you pursue your attack, in such a way that you do not retreat when tori starts his or her aikido technique, nor should you just get limp and give in to it. Instead, make sure to keep your aim and focus on uke all through. This way, you remain in contact, so that there is something for tori to work on.

The essence of the attack is not the method by which it is done, its physical expression, but the intent of uke – the direction of uke's effort, from within his or her own body to the inner of tori's body. This line or flow of intention, which can be called *ki*, is what tori really has to work on by re-directing it. If you halt your attack and turn away – either concretely or just in your mind – then this flow stops, and tori has nothing to work on.

This is not at all the same as giving in voluntarily to the aikido technique. Actually, it is quite the contrary. Any attacker knows that the only way to succeed is to pursue. The attacking spirit must continue, or it will fail. So, in aikido you pursue your attack, for tori to do aikido on 'the real thing.'

This is very well understood in all the attacking martial arts. You must pursue, in order for your attack to succeed, but also so that you keep some kind of guard all through. If you halt your attack and turn away, you are an open target to any counterattack.

So, keep your aim at tori, as long as you can. Again, don't make this a contest of any kind between tori's powers and yours. Do it in the spirit of giving tori a sincere attack to handle, but do allow tori to handle it.

Posture

Most of the basics that apply to uke when attacking are the same as what tori should consider in the aikido defense. This is certainly true for the importance of having a good posture.

Uke as well as tori should strive to have a straight posture all through the attack and the following aikido technique. Uke will lose his or her posture somewhere in the process of the defense technique, but this should not be voluntarily. It should be caused by tori's action.

At the outset, uke's posture should be absolutely straight and almost exactly vertical. Not completely vertical, though. There is a slight leaning forward, almost invisible, because of uke's aim and focus forward. But do not try to accomplish this consciously – that will be too much. Just let it happen naturally. If you find that you lean too much forward, so that your balance weakens, make sure to correct it.

This slight leaning forward happens naturally as soon as you intend to move forward. You can notice it by first

Chudankamae, middle guard, with sword against sword, at the usual maai starting distance. Seminar in Stockholm. Photo by Magnus Burman.

standing straight on the spot, and then prepare to take a step forward. When you do that, your body will first lean in that direction, maybe just an inch or two. The weight of your body moves from the heels of your feet toward the toes. It is the change of balance that is automatic when you prepare to go to action.

If you start moving without this slight initial leaning forward, you will have less balance and less forward force. You will not be able to move quickly and decisively.

Standing straight might be a problem, because we normally allow ourselves to have a bad posture for lengths of time – particularly when we sit down in chairs. To improve your posture, lie down of the floor now and then. Lie on your back with your arms by your sides, your legs straight, and your head in such an angle that your chin approaches your chest. This will straighten your back.

Try to remain in that posture when you stand up. Repeat the very simple exercise as much as you need to, in order to improve your posture.

A straight posture increases your sense of authority and

Aikido

power. Others feel it, too. It is very helpful to you, also outside of the *dojo*, the practice hall.

When tori commences the aikido technique, you will at some point lose your posture. This is part of tori's breaking your balance, which is necessary for most aikido techniques. Don't resist frantically, but don't lose your posture voluntarily. It should be the doing of tori.

Kamae　構

Kamae is the Japanese word for guard. A correct posture, described above, is the first and most important aspect of it. Without a good posture, you cannot have a trustworthy guard position.

Next is awareness. You should be relaxed but still attentive, ready to spring into action. You focus on tori, but not to the extent that you lose your initiative or independence. Focusing too hard on somebody sort of makes you his or her slave, so that you no longer can control your impulses. Keep your integrity.

The proper kamae awareness includes respect for tori. In the martial arts, you should never have the attitude of expecting tori only to do what was preordained, for example a certain aikido technique. It is better to have the mind of facing an actual enemy, not knowing how he or she will react. This way, you will learn to make your attacks believable and reasonable, not like just running right into the fire.

Only if you behave like an attacker would, tori can learn to guide and control you properly, which includes creating reactions in you through *atemi*, the distraction strike, and other sophisticated manipulations of your impulses. This becomes possible when you have an attitude of respect for tori, acknowledging his or her ability to strike first or to counterstrike.

Don't overdo this. You don't want to start an actual fight. But try anyway to have this awareness.

You should start from a proper distance. This 間合 is called *maai* in Japanese. The pictogram for the word shows a swinging door, like those to cowboy saloons.

The gap between the swinging sections of the door should be such that they neither hit one another, nor leave too much open space. They should fit. It is the same with the distance between uke and tori, before the attack.

If you stand too close to tori, none of you has a chance to react to a sudden attack – so none of you would want to be in that position. If you stand too far away, you have no way of attacking tori without him or her easily avoiding it. You have to find the perfect mean.

A simple rule for a good maai is that by just one step – neither more nor less – you should be close enough to reach tori with your attack. This means that you need to adapt your distance depending on what attack you plan, and if you are armed or not. Other circumstances may also influence your distance. For example, if one of you has a longer reach than the other, or if you adapt a certain stance that affects your reach.

In aikido, it is very common to always be in *hanmigamae*, the angled kamae where one side of your body is turned slightly forward. Both uke and tori tend to do this. I would not recommend it. If tori stands in hanmigamae before the attack comes, a lot about tori's strategy is revealed, so that uke can counter it. If uke begins in hanmigamae it is really a defensive guard, and not the best for initiating an attack.

Uke should have a straight guard in the beginning, and tori should do the same, facing uke straight on. Uke might slip into the hanmi angle of the body in the actual attack. Some attack forms allow for that. And tori surely turns to hanmi already at the evasive *taisabaki* step. But none of them gains from beginning with that stance.

Overall, uke should adapt stances that have the attitude of the attacker. That is usually straight on, with a persisting spirit forward. It is an offensive mind, not a defensive one, and it should remain all through the aikido technique.

Chudan maegeri, middle level front kick, at a seminar in Pardubice, Czech Republic. Photo by Leos Matousek.

Functionality

Attacks in aikido must be believable, in the way that somebody skilled in the martial arts would be likely to pursue with some confidence. Therefore, they have to be functional.

Grips should be applied in a way that makes sense to an attacker who strives to get control of the defender, without getting obviously open to counterattacks. In that sense, grips are both attacks and guards: they aim to limit the defender's ability to get away, and at the same time to stop the defender from striking back at the attacker.

For example, a wrist grip should be applied from above, and not from the side or from below, to effectively stop tori from moving the arm upward, toward uke's belly, neck, or face. A shoulder grip should be applied to the side of the shoulder, and not on top of it, to limit as much as possible tori's ability to move the arm. Two-handed grips should be made in such a way that uke is reasonably protected from counterattacks, although both of uke's arms are occupied by the grips.

Strikes should be done in a distinct manner, at such a distance that they would actually reach if tori remained on the spot. In aikido there is no meaning to use safety distance with strikes, so that they would not hit if tori remained. In such training, tori has no chance of learning proper timing, distance, and movement.

A better measure of safety is to start practicing defense against strikes in a slow speed, increasing it gradually as tori gets more comfortable in the response.

Strikes should also be aimed at meaningful targets on tori's body. These targets differ depending on the attack form used. Some strikes may seem completely useless, such as the *shomenuchi* open hand strike at the top of tori's head – but that is really a symbolic sword attack, done unarmed for safety reasons, and for understanding the basics of aikido evasions.

The best way to learn functional attack techniques is to keep in mind: what would the attacker do to ensure success? Attacks should be competent, and they should be done when the situation creates reasonable openings for them. If tori has both arms in front, there is no meaning in trying *ushiro ryotedori*, grabbing tori's wrists from behind. If tori holds up both hands in a confident guard position, a strike is not as likely to succeed as for example quickly grabbing the wrist that is the closest to uke. And so on.

Apply some strategic thinking when you are the attacker, so that you attack becomes probable. Also, this way tori has a chance of learning how to manipulate uke to do certain attacks, by creating openings for them.

Unbendable arm
The unbendable arm is frequently used by both the attacker and the defender, so it deserves some comment. The expression is used for the extended arm position used in just about every aikido technique, either during moments of it or all through. The arm is not completely extended, because that would make the elbow weak and vulnerable. Instead, it is held at a slight curve, sort of the same as that of *katana*, the Japanese sword. You should have energy all through the arm, making it very difficult for anyone else to bend.

Jan Hermansson, 7 dan Aikikai, shows osae, pinning, using the unbendable arm. Seminar in Plzen, Czech Republic. Photo by Antonín Knízek.

This extended, slightly curved arm form is not only used in aikido, but in most Japanese martial arts. For example, it is used in judo when the opponents hold each other by the shoulders, like the aikido attack *ryokatadori*. It is used constantly in the sword grip of kendo and iaido. It is used in karatedo when doing *tsuki*, the basic fist strike, where the arm should not extend more, or the elbow might get damaged. And on and on. You find it just about everywhere in *budo*, the Japanese martial arts.

Therefore, it is also used a lot by the attacker in aikido. Most of the grips should be done with unbendable arms, which serve both as making the grips the strongest, and as protection against counterattacks from tori. The unbendable arm is used in most of the strikes, too, for maximum effect.

In some attacks, the unbendable arm is particularly obvious. The *shomenuchi* strike is one of them. The *katatedori* grip is another. But it is present, more or less, in just about every attack. Pay attention to it, and your attack techniques will improve.

You can train the unbendable arm. A common exercise for it in aikido is to put your forearm on top of your partner's shoulder, and he or she will try to bend your arm. Don't fight it, but focus forward in the direction of your arm, way beyond its reach, as if pointing intensely at something far away. This extended focus will make your arm much stronger, and quite difficult for somebody else to bend.

Your whole posture will benefit from properly extended unbendable arms. So will your attitude and confidence.

Precision
It is by increasing the precision in your attacks that you really make them improve. Perfect your posture. Pay attention to the unbendable arm mentioned above. Also, work on the angle of your wrist. In all grips it should be such that the hand is held at an upward angle from the forearm. It is the same in the sword grip. Use your fingers correctly. In both grips and strikes, you should have the most strength in your little finger, and practically none in your index finger.

There are many other details to consider in the attack forms. Continue to explore them, and strive always to perfect your attacking techniques.

Precision is also needed in the rhythm of your movements. You should find the optimal timing between the advancing step and the grip or strike. For the beginner it is best to do one thing at a time: first the step, then the grip or strike. But in an advanced manner, the grip or strike is done right before your advancing foot lands on the floor.

Steps, by the way, should also be considered. Many aikido students drag their feet on *tatami*, the mat, confident of its smooth surface. But that does not foster the proper awareness. The feet should touch the floor so lightly when advancing, that any obstacle can be avoided without problem. And lift your toes a bit when moving a foot forward. That way you will not stumble on a small unevenness on the floor, or get toes stuck in a crack between two mats.

Bend your knees to increase balance and stability – when you stand in a guard, as well as when you move your legs. Low stances are recommended for the beginners, but also to prefer on an advanced level. As you improve, you

Christian Tissier, 7 dan Aikikai, attacked with morotedori, a two-handed wrist grip. Seminar in Stockholm. Photo by Magnus Hartmann.

will find the right height of your stance for what you do. It differs depending on what attack form you choose.

Think of where you look, and how you do it. If you stare too much, you are far too easy to read, giving away your movements before you make them, and you lose ability to adapt to surprises. On the other hand, if you don't look where you go, you will make all kinds of mistakes.

Advanced attacks should be done in a surprising way. You may stand in a guard that shows what you are about to do, but no preliminary movement or change of expression should reveal when you do it. The best way to learn this is by striving to surprise yourself. Get ready for the attack, and sort of leave for your body to choose the moment to do it. If it is not a conscious decision, it will be very difficult for the defender to spot beforehand.

You also need to be able to move forward without any initial backward movement. For example, if you intend to strike with a forward punch, don't begin by pulling the arm slightly backward right before you charge. And make sure that your initial stance is such that you don't need to shift your balance over to your back leg to be able to pounce. Your initial guard position should be like a tightened spring: your muscles are prepared, and your balance is already good for leaping forward.

The things mentioned above all need a level of precision. You will improve by training. Just make sure that you pay attention to the details, instead of just attacking as a service to tori. In aikido every attack is doomed to fail. Still, you should work wholeheartedly on perfecting them. That is the only way you can help your partner and yourself toward perfecting your aikido techniques.

Center 丹田

Something of fundamental importance in the Japanese martial arts is *tanden*, the center. It is a point inside the body, approximately two inches below the navel. In Indian tradition, it is one of the seven major *chakra* – the second one, called *Svadhisthana*, the dwelling of the I. Chinese and Japanese tradition describe it as a source of power, and therefore the point from which all movements shall emerge.

It is also the body's center of mass.

The pictogram for tanden (or *dantian* in Chinese) consists of the sign for the color red and that for a rice field. The red rice field, a symbol of vast resources of life-giving substances. It has a lot of symbolic meanings, and becomes sort of a compass in the continued development of one's aikido, but for the purposes of this book we settle for its importance and use in attacks.

You need to anchor your balance and stability in your center. This makes sense, since it is your body's center of mass, but also because it is the source to a powerful *ki* flow. You find more about ki below.

When you do your attacks, you should foster the idea of them coming from your center, and remaining in contact with it. When you strike, it should feel like it starts in your center, deep within your body, and extends forward somewhat like the flow of water through a fireman's hose. This flow from your center onto tori is the essence of the attack, whatever striking technique you use, and it is this flow that

Tomas Ohlsson at the author's dojo Enighet, in chudankamae, the middle sword guard, where the sword is held in front of tanden, the center. Photo by Stefan Stenudd.

tori needs to accept and redirect in the aikido technique. Your body will follow this flow, because it is committed to it.

Also your grip attacks need to be extensions from your center, with a flow remaining as long as the grip is applied. Whatever part of tori's body you grip, try to make it feel like you control him or her with the flow of energy from your center, through the grip, and into the center of tori. That is the essence of any grip attack.

Now, the hand is such that if you tighten your index finger, you can notice that the shoulder muscles tighten as well. Muscularly, as well as in your mind, the index finger is kind of connected to the shoulders. If you tighten your little finger instead, you will feel the link to your center much more clearly.

More than any of the other fingers, the little finger is connected to your center. So, when you grip somebody, or when you tighten your hand into a fist – have the most power in your little finger, and don't worry much about the others.

This leads to the strongest and most powerful attack technique. It also makes you the most balanced and stable, all through. If you have a highly centered grip, tori really has to do the technique correctly to get out of it. And if you strike with your center, you develop great force – so please take care, so that no one gets hurt.

When you develop your attack techniques, it should feel more and more like the center is doing all the work, and the rest of the body is quite relaxed.

Being properly centered is also the way to be able to spring forward without additional preparation. You have immediate access to your bodily powers. When you stand in guard, preparing for the attack, make sure to focus on your center. You will soon discover that you hardly need any other preparation than that.

Also your posture is dependent on your center. Instead of trying to fix your posture with a number of muscular corrections, which only leads to a kind of mayhem within your body, make yourself sort of grow from your center. If you use deep belly breathing, which I would like to call center breathing, your body will sort of rise from the inside, and your posture will improve automatically.

Ki

Center breathing is belly breathing, also called diaphragm breathing. It is very effective breathing for getting lots of oxygen into your system. It is also the way to get a powerful *ki* flow. Among the Chinese and the Japanese, the center is regarded as the inner ocean of ki, the life energy.

The idea of a kind of life energy linked to air and breathing can also be found in many cultures and traditions outside China and Japan. In India it is called *prana*, in the old Greek tradition *pneuma*, in Hebrew tradition *ruach*, in Latin *spiritus*, and so on.

The Chinese and Japanese pictogram for it shows rice and steam – boiling rice, the way to make their main nutri-

Morihei Ueshiba (1883-1969), founder of aikido, makes a throw without body contact, using ki, in his late years. Among aikidoists, he is usually called kaiso, *founder, or* osensei, *great teacher. His grandson Moriteru Ueshiba is the present doshu, leader of the art, at Aikikai headquarters, Hombu Dojo in Tokyo. Photo courtesy of Yasuo Kobayashi.*

tion edible. That is indeed a way of marking its importance. It also shows a connection to *tanden*, the center, the pictogram of which denotes a red rice field.

Ki emanates from the center. You stimulate it by belly breathing, and by focusing on your center. Also, activity with an aim improves the flow. I like to explain ki as the ether of intention. It is the energy by which you do something, accomplish something, move somewhere. So, of course it is of great importance in the martial arts.

Whatever attack you make, the ki flow of it is the essence, and what tori should primarily relate to in the aikido technique. As soon as you take aim at tori, long before you actually charge, there is a ki flow from you to tori, since it is the ether of intention. It really means that tori's aikido response can start as soon as uke takes aim – but that's quite advanced, and not the topic of this book. Anyway, it does demand sharp and skilled uke attacks.

If you become aware of the ki flow that commenced when you took aim, and focus on that all through, you will find that your attacks get more distinct, powerful, and precise. Trust your intention, and the rest will practically take care of itself.

You don't have to believe in the existence of ki as a life energy, in order to use it. See it as a symbol for mental training and a help for your concentration. Whatever the case, focusing on the ki flow will improve your skills.

When you grip tori, it should feel like your ki is penetrating tori's body, through the contact of the grip, and sort of imprisoning tori's center, snaring its ki. When you strike, you should feel like you do it first with your ki flow, and the hand or foot or weapon just follows that trace. For a powerful strike, it is important to send your ki flow right through tori, and not just on to his or her body.

When you have practiced it for some time, you will be quite aware of both your own ki flow and that of your partner. It will make aikido and its techniques much more clear to you.

Aikido

Getting out of kubishime, at the author's dojo.

Ukemi

受身

This book is not about falling techniques, *ukemi*, but some things need to be said about the attacker's attitude once tori has commenced the aikido technique. You need to remain in the attacker spirit. That way you can feel how the aikido techniques really work.

Aikido throws are such that uke falls because of the attack, or to be more precise: the intention behind the attack. When you have made a commitment to an attack, you are sort of locked into it until your body becomes clearly aware of its failure. Without this lasting commitment, no attack would have a chance to succeed.

Tori uses this commitment, and thereby guides uke to another outcome than the one intended with the attack. Through the technique, uke is given no other choice but to persist with the attacking spirit, continuing with the aim at tori. There is no opportunity to retreat from it, and doing so would anyway expose uke to more serious counterattacks. All the way to the actual throw, uke is locked into the technique – because tori uses uke's intention and aim.

The actual fall, *ukemi*, is partly the result of training. Uke is trained to make a safe fall, so this is what the body automatically chooses when tori makes the throw. Others might instead stumble away uncontrollably, and probably still land on the ground. The controlled ukemi fall is not only the safest way out, but also the quickest way to get back into a stable guard position.

Something similar is taking place in the pinning techniques. Uke is guided into them without much of a choice anywhere through them. Since the attacker mind is a combination of continued attacking spirit, and a sense of protection, a guard, this is used by tori in the movements leading to the pinning. Uke's best protection, and best chance of getting out of it, is by persisting with the aim and the attacking spirit. Switching to something else would just expose uke to much graver risks.

This natural way of handling an attack is one way by

Kokyunage at the author's dojo.

Nobuyoshi Tamura, 8 dan Aikikai, shows mae ukemi, forward fall, at a 2008 seminar in the author's dojo Enighet, when he was 75 years old. Photo by Anders Heinonen.

which this martial art is doing away with fighting as such. This was the idea of Morihei Ueshiba, the founder of aikido. Both for tori and uke, the aikido technique is the safest way out. So, uke doesn't feel beaten, but saved. Actually, the more focused and committed your attack is, the clearer this becomes to you.

KOGEKI

攻撃

Attacks in Aikido

Aikido

Aihanmi relation 合半身

Aihanmi katatedori
Shomenuchi
Shomenate
Tsuki
Maegeri

Aihanmi relation
The aihanmi relation is when both persons have the same foot and arm forward. This is the traditional and typical guard between two adversaries in almost any martial art. Most right-handed persons want to stand with their left leg and arm forward in unarmed combat. In the sword arts, though, it is usually the right side forward.

Since aikido has so many similarities to the sword arts, practitioners normally prefer the right side, like the basic *kendo* (Japanese fencing) guard position. But it is important to develop equal skills for both sides.

The aihanmi relation is sometimes referred to as *kosa*, cross over, because of the diagonal position of tori's and uke's guard.

Aihanmi katatedori
Aihanmi katatedori (also called *kosadori*) is a right hand grip of tori's right wrist, or a left hand grip of tori's left wrist. In the basic form, the same hand and foot should be forward in the stance of both tori and uke.

You get the best posture and relation to the partner if you compare it to the *chudankamae* sword guard. Extend your hand from your center (*tanden*), not to the side, and face tori straight on.

Think of it as an initial attack, fully alert, which can easily be followed up by other attacks.

It is very important not to think of it as only a grip of tori's wrist, but as a connection to control his or her whole body. You grip the arm, but you focus on tori's whole body, in particular his or her center. There should be a fairly straight line from your center, through the grip, to tori's center.

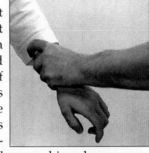

Your grip on tori's wrist should also be very similar to that on a sword. There should be a sharp angle between your hand and forearm, with the back of your hand up and your fingers down. Some people grip from the side or even from below. That is much weaker and less of a protection, since it allows for tori to easily move his or her arm up, toward your face.

You should not press down or any other direction, but hold so that every direction is equally difficult for tori to move the hand.

When it comes to the roles of the fingers, again the grip is like that on a sword. Concentrate on gripping with your little finger, and don't worry about the rest of the fingers. This way, your grip will be anchored in your center. If you grip with the most force in your index finger, your shoulder will stiffen and you will lose the connection between your center and your grip.

A good way of describing the ideal grip on a wrist (as well as on a sword) is to think that the little finger pulls the wrist into the palm of your hand. When your palm is tightly connected to tori's wrist, sort of air tight, then your control of tori through the grip is optimal.

This attack form is unreasonably neglected in many aikido dojos. It may seem almost awkward as a grip, compared to *gyakuhanmi* (where the right hand grabs the left, or vice versa), but the aihanmi relation is by far the most common between adversaries in any other martial art. With the grip, you have a clear and concrete way of getting familiar with this relation.

You may also be surprised by how practical it can be as an attack. For example, when your opponent stands in a karate or boxing style guard, you can quite easily snap the opponent's wrist, which is a good start to penetrate his or her guard.

Shomenuchi

Shomenuchi is a strike to the top of tori's head, with an open hand. It is done as a symbol of a sword attack. It would not make much sense to hit a person's skull with the bare hand.

The hand is *tegatana* (hand sword, called *shuto* in karatedo), with the little finger side as the sword's edge. The relation to tori is of aihanmi nature, because both have the same foot forward in the basic form. Also, uke has the same foot forward as the striking hand.

In the shomenuchi strike, it is good to hold the other hand slightly behind the striking one, so as to resemble the two-handed sword grip used on *katana*, the Japanese sword. This also helps you to remain centered through the attack. The strike should be done with the whole arm, extended in the unbendable arm fashion, and not just the forearm – again to resemble the sword cut.

Lift the hand above your head, like the *jodankamae* (high guard) position with the sword, but don't do that before advancing toward tori. To advance in a jodankamae position gives less protection than to do so in *chudankamae* (middle guard, in front of your center). You raise the hand at the end of your final step toward tori, so that the strike follows almost immediately.

Don't relax the striking hand, but stiffen it – especially the little finger, so that the hand side muscle hardens. Otherwise the hand is quite fragile in such a strike. Remember also to approach to actual striking distance. Tori cannot learn timing and distance properly, if the strike is done too far away, where it would not reach tori even if he or she remained on the spot.

I have noticed that many aikido practitioners shift their front hand in their shomenuchi attack, so that they start with one hand in front but do the strike with the other. This is simply not possible when you hold a sword – you would just strike yourself with it (try it, if you  don't believe me). Therefore, I strongly recommend that you keep the same hand forward through the attack. If you begin with your right hand forward, then that is the hand you strike with.

In the Japanese sword arts, you never shift your sword grip. You always hold your sword with the left hand at the base, closest to your body, and the right hand in front, near *tsuba* (the sword guard). In aikido, though, we happily shift positions of the hands, as if completely ambidextrous. That is actually the idea. We should practice ambidextrously, so that one side works as well as the other.

Of course, the shomenuchi attack has no meaning when done with an unarmed hand. The head is hard, especially at the forehead, so there is no hand that can hit it without more damage being done to the hand than to tori's head. This is simply a way of training aikido in a safe way against the sword attack, or any other armed attack to the head from above.

Shomenate
Shomenate is a strike to tori's face, with the side of the hand. It is done as a symbol of a sword or knife forward strike (*tsuki*). The relation to tori is of aihanmi nature, because both

have the same foot forward, in the basic form. Also, uke has the same foot forward as the striking hand. In this attack (just like with *shomenuchi*) it is recommendable to hold the other hand slightly behind the striking one, so as to resemble the two-handed sword grip. Begin from *chudankamae* (middle guard, in front of your center), and thrust the hand forward and upward, toward tori's face.

This is not really a basic attack form in aikido, but it is anyway used quite frequently in training – often as a substitute for shomenuchi, which is unfortunate, since the two attacks cannot always be treated the same way by tori. It is also frequently used by tori as an *atemi* (distraction strike).

Some aikido schools practice in such a way that tori initiates by doing shomenate toward uke, who blocks with the same movement. Tori then does the technique on uke's blocking arm. I am not too fond of that, since it actually makes tori the attacker. This is contrary to the firm aikido principle of defense only.

Make sure to stiffen the hand, just like with shomenuchi, and make sure that you advance so that you reach an actual striking distance. Use the idea of the unbendable arm to make the attack strong.

Unlike shomenuchi, this attack is meaningful even when done unarmed. You only need to change the angle and aim of the hand to make it a very effective attack indeed. Turn it sideways and aim for the throat or the nose, and you have a very effective attack form. It must be used with caution.

For tori, this attack is interesting as it tends to sneak up, because of its trajectory and the fact that it is done with the forward hand of uke's guard. It can also be practiced instead of *tsuki*, the fist punch, by aikido students who are not yet enough familiar with the aikido techniques to handle them against forceful and quick striking attacks. Still, it should be regarded with respect, since it is not as innocent an attack as it may seem.

Tsuki

Tsuki is a fist strike either to the face (*jodantsuki*) or to the solar plexus (*chudantsuki*). It needs to be trained substantially before it becomes a good attack for tori to defend against with aikido techniques. Much more can be said about it than what there is room for here. In *karatedo* the constant training of tsuki can be compared to the training of the basic cut in the sword arts. It takes years to learn well.

A few pointers:

The power of the strike lies in the acceleration of it, according to Newton's law of mechanics: The force is equal the mass times the acceleration in square. So, the acceleration is far more important than the size and weight of the attacker. Notice also that it is not the speed, but the increase of it, that makes for the power of the strike.

Acceleration is accomplished by relaxing in the movement, to harden your fist and arm only at impact. For stability, the direction of the strike must be straight, and end so that the fist is directly in line with your center. This means that you need to angle your body a bit, but not much, so that the body side of the striking arm is slightly more forward than the other. This body turn is done so that it adds force to the strike.

Moreover, the index finger and middle finger base knuckles are aimed straight at the target, so that they hit first. Form the fist by closing your little finger the most firmly. The other fingers are not nearly as important (just like in a sword grip).

Do not tighten up your index finger forcefully, or your shoulders will get stiff. Make sure that the thumb is tightly connected to the fist, for its protection.

The fist is held in an angle that prevents the wrist from bending on impact. This angle is such that the two knuckles to hit first are in line with the forearm. You can easily test your fist angle by pressing it on to a wall. You will notice the increased stability at the correct angle.

In traditional karatedo, the fist rotates 180° during the strike – from fingers up to fingers down. This increases stability and effect (somewhat like the spinning bullet from a gun). At impact, the hand has turned 90°, and the re-

maining 90° turn happens at the remainder of the strike.

At full extension of the tsuki, there should be a 90° angle between the arm and the body, again for stability. The arm should not be completely stretched, since that can damage the elbow when you miss the target (and you should miss, if tori is doing *taisabaki*, the evasive movement, properly). Use the unbendable arm form, where a slight curve of the arm remains.

Remember to advance so that tsuki would really reach tori properly, if he or she were to stay on the spot. Otherwise tori has no chance of learning the right timing and distance. When you advance, don't strike until you have reached tori, i.e. at the end of your last step.

Strive for good balance and a straight posture at the end of your tsuki. If tori makes the aikido technique properly, you will lose your posture and balance, but you should not do that voluntarily. It has to be accomplished by tori.

There are two basic forms of tsuki in karatedo, depending on the foot position compared to that of the striking arm. *Oitsuki* is where the foot forward is the same as the striking arm. This is the most used tsuki in aikido.

In some aikido dojos no other tsuki is ever trained. Surely, this is because the arm and foot relation here is the same as in the most common sword techniques and gripping techniques. In aikido it is rare to attack with the opposite foot forward, for reasons of balance and reach (and habit).

However, in karatedo the most appreciated tsuki is *gyakutsuki*, where the forward foot is the opposite from the striking arm. If you strike with your right arm, then the left foot is forward, and vice

versa. Gyakutsuki is very practical and popular in *kumite*, karate competition, because by this you can approach the opponent slightly to the side and thereby avoid his or her counterattack.

I think that aikido students should practice gyakutsuki as well as oitsuki – because it's there. Also, it is good to exercise because uke ends up in a slightly different position from that of oitsuki. This is particularly evident with the feet. Some aikido techniques take for granted that the same arm and leg are forward. They can become awkward when this is not the case. That needs to be experienced.

Maegeri

Aikido works fine also against kick attacks, but in most dojos this is rarely trained, simply because kicks are rarely trained. Most kicks are quite difficult to learn, and the time at hand in aikido practice is just not enough – considering the many other things, deemed more important, that the aikido students need to exercise.
So, many dojos simply exclude kicks altogether.

That is a pity. It gives the impression that the aikido principles don't apply to kick attacks, which is wrong. A martial art with defense techniques even against knife and sword attacks, would not be without means against kicks.

Another disadvantage of not practicing aikido techniques against kicks is that the practitioners fail to relate safely and correctly to the attacker's guard position and attacking options. If you don't know about kicks, you don't see them coming, and you don't position yourself so that you avoid them.

It is true that some kicks are far too time consuming to master, but others are actually rather easy to learn sufficiently for the practice of aikido defense against them to be meaningful. The most basic karatedo kick, *maegeri*, is one of them.

Maegeri is a straight front kick, either to the belly (*chudan maegeri*) or to the head (*jodan maegeri*). The former does not even demand any particular agility. Therefore, at least the chudan maegeri should be included as a basic attack form in aikido.

I sort it among the aihanmi relation attacks because of its basic nature, and because those who practice karatedo prefer the aihanmi relation to their opponent, where both stand with the same leg forward. The arms have similar positions. The kick is usually done with the leg that is to the back in the initial guard.

Start by leaning over on your front foot, while you pull the back leg knee up toward your chest. Don't swing the leg forward, but raise the knee high. Then you push your foot forward in the actual kick. This way, the foot moves horizontally toward tori's belly, which is the direction that gives the kick the most power.

Your toes should be turned upward, as much as you can, so that it is the hard base of them (the ball) that hits the target, instead of the much weaker toes.

As you kick, your arms switch positions, so that the arm on the same side as your kicking leg ends up being the forward one. This is natural, so it is what the body wants to do. It is also the best protection against counterattacks.

Make sure that you are actually close enough to tori for your kick to reach properly. Be cautious when you are learning this, and if tori is inexperienced with defense against kicks.

What is true for any other attack is also true for kicks: you must be balanced and centered, and make the kick as an extension of energy from your center. You must aim well and let your spirit extend far beyond the target, for the kick to be precise and strong.

If you want to try the high kick, *jodan maegeri*, there is a simple trick to compensate for insufficient agility: lean backward. If your upper body leans backward, you can easily reach much higher with your kick. Try it, and you will be surprised.

Never compensate limited agility with stretching your other leg, or going up on your toes with the supporting foot. You will get hopelessly out of stability, so the kick will just make you stumble backward if you actually hit with it. Just like all other attack forms, kicking is best done from a low position, even if you are not agile. You can lean backward with your whole torso, but you should not get up on your toes. The former does not lessen your stability much, but the latter sure does.

Aikido

Gyakuhanmi relation 逆半身

Gyakuhanmi katatedori
Ryotedori
Katadori
Ryokatadori
Munedori
Sodedori
Ryosodedori
Ryohijidori
Yokomenuchi
Katadori menuchi
Kata katatedori
Yokotsuki
Mawashigeri

Gyakuhanmi relation

The gyakuhanmi relation is when tori and uke have opposite legs forward. Either tori has the left leg and uke the right leg forward, or vice versa. This can happen in any martial art when a right-handed person meets a left-handed one. Otherwise, it is very rare in martial arts involving strikes or kicks. This is particularly awkward for right-handed persons, since they are in a vast majority and therefore have little experience of it.

In a gripping attack, though, gyakuhanmi is the most common relation, since it comes quite naturally when you grab someone.

Gyakuhanmi katatedori

Gyakuhanmi katatedori is when uke grabs tori's nearest wrist. Either uke's right hand grabs tori's left wrist, or the left hand grabs the right wrist. In the basic form, their foot positions have the same relation: when uke grabs with the right hand, his or her right foot is forward, while tori's left foot and arm are forward.

This grip is the most common in aikido – so much so that it is usually just called katatedori. Gyakuhanmi is taken for granted. Indeed, it is the most convenient way to grab an opponent's wrist, but the gyakuhanmi relation between the two is not common in other martial arts, where the *aihanmi* relation is almost always the case. Therefore, I am not sure that gyakuhanmi should be allowed such a dominant role in training – they are both needed. Aihanmi must also be studied properly.

Anyway, regarding the grip itself, it should be done in very much the same way as aihanmi katatedori. The little finger is the most important one, holding on the hardest. The angle and position of the hand is the same as in aihanmi. So is the tight contact with the palm on tori's wrist, the  spirit forward without any pushing, the extension of the arm in the unbendable arm fashion, and so on. See the text on aihanmi katatedori above, for more on these details.

The difference from aihanmi katatedori is that gyakuhanmi is by necessity off center. Both for uke and tori, the grip is to the side of the body, not straight in front of it. Still, it is necessary to feel the connection with the center, and not to regard the grip as something applied from the shoulder down. Also, uke should apply the grip as an initial and not a final attack. That means alertness and a continued focus on tori.

An important key to understanding the gyakuhanmi relation as well as its katatedori application, lies in carefully considering the potential of the free hand – of both uke and tori. If this is neglected, the attack is of little meaning, and so is practicing aikido techniques on it.

Ryotedori

Ryotedori is when uke grabs both of tori's wrists. It can simply be described as a double *gyakuhanmi katatedori*, and what goes for the latter applies also here. Since ryotedori is connected to gyakuhanmi, the stance of uke and tori should relate in the same way – that is, if one has the left foot forward, the other should have the right foot forward, and vice versa.

An interesting aspect of ryotedori, and some other two-handed grips, is the deviation from a single line connection with the center. Here, both uke and tori are so to say split, in regard to their center. Uke must still make the grips with extension of power from the center, and still regard the grips as means to control tori's center.

Because of this split from the center, I would say that ryotedori relates more to *jo* (the staff) than to *ken* (the sword). On the staff, the hands are usually separated, and should be able to move freely up and down the full length of the staff. One should still be able to maintain one's center, and to fetch the source of each movement from there.

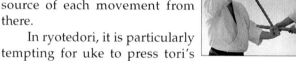

In ryotedori, it is particularly tempting for uke to press tori's hands downward, but this is a flawed attack with many weaknesses – the weakened guard against counterattacks being just one of them. Don't push or pull in any direction. Maintain the position. That's what tori has to work with.

For exercising the awareness of both uke and tori, it is also good to carefully consider the potential of the legs in this position. The arms are locked in the grips, but the legs are not. So, both tori and uke should pay attention to the other's ability to kick or use the legs in other ways.

Katadori

Katadori is a grip of tori's *keikogi* (training jacket) by the shoulder. Uke should have the same foot forward as the hand gripping tori. The stance is a gyakuhanmi relation, which means that if uke stands with the left foot forward, then tori has the right foot forward, and vice versa.

When you grab tori's dress, make sure that it is done mostly with your little finger, which anchors the grip in your center and makes you more flexible than if done with the most power in the index finger.

Don't let your thumb get too nestled into the cloth of tori's jacket. Actually, you should be careful about all your fingers, since some aikido techniques really tie them into tori's jacket in a way that might harm them during the technique.

Keep your elbow pointing downward, to have the best stability and control in the grip. Also, make sure to use the unbendable arm extension.

Some aikido practitioners tend to grip on top of the shoulder, instead of to the side of it. This is rather meaningless, since it is very difficult to control tori that way. The grip should limit tori's ability to use the arm, which is not accomplished at all with a top shoulder grip. Only when you hold by the side of the shoulder, on the upper arm, you are able to have some control of tori's arm.

Of course, the grip should be done in the spirit of being an initial attack. Maintain readiness to continue with other attack forms (like in *katadori menuchi*, described below). There is no passive attack form in aikido, so uke should always remain alert.

For tori, katadori is particularly interesting because of the strength of this grip, making it very difficult to escape. Also, some of the aikido techniques are quite awkward and complicated to do on this attack form.

Ryokatadori

Ryokatadori is when uke grips tori's jacket by both shoulders, so it is simply a double *katadori*. The stance is of the gyakuhanmi kind, which means that if uke stands with the left foot forward, then tori has the right foot forward, and vice versa.

Grab in the same way as described above about katadori – mainly with the little finger, careful not to get your fingers too much nestled into the cloth of tori's jacket, and by the sides of the shoulders instead of on top of them.

In this position you really need to be able to control tori's arms to some extent, since both of your own arms are occupied by the grip you applied. For example, if tori tries to hit you, you should be able to block it without letting go of tori's shoulders.

The grip should be done in the spirit of being an initial attack, with a readiness to continue with other attack forms – like a kick, or by pulling or pushing tori. Actually, it is not a very practical attack at all, if not some continued attack move is intended.

Notice that this attack needs you to face tori straight on, to have good control. Avoid any *hanmigamae* turn of your body (hanmigamae is when you stand with one side of your body slightly more forward than the other). Notice also that this is an attack form which is a bit awkward to apply if tori stands in an accentuated hanmigamae. Therefore, it makes the most sense if tori, too, stands straight forward.

The difficulties that tori has to solve when attacked by ryokatadori are quite the same as with katadori – but doubled. Without knowing the proper body movements, tori can really get stuck in this grip.

Munedori

Munedori (sometimes spelled *mu-nadori*) is when uke grips tori's jacket by the front, right on the chest. Because of its similarity with *katadori*, the stance is a gyakuhanmi relation, which means that if uke stands with the left foot forward, then tori has the right foot forward, and vice versa. Uke should stand with the same foot forward as the hand doing the grip, for maximum stability.

Do the grabbing in the same way as described above about katadori – mainly with the little finger, careful not to get your fingers too much nestled into the cloth of tori's jacket. Your hand should be positioned so that your little finger is down and your thumb up. This keeps a good link to your center. Your elbow points downward. When your elbow is down, tori will have the most difficulty in applying a technique on your arm. Use the unbendable arm extension, for the best control.

Also, try to apply the grip directly with just one hand – don't start by adjusting the collar of tori's jacket with the other hand. If you do, then tori should really act on the first hand coming, and not wait for the next one.

The grip should be done in the spirit of being an initial attack, with a readiness to continue with other attack forms.

What makes this attack particularly interesting for tori is its firmness. Correctly applied, this grip is not easy to get out of. An additional difficulty is the fact that tori doesn't have too much room for applying an aikido technique, since uke is blocking much of the space in front of tori.

This is an attack form which is a bit awkward to apply if tori stands in an accentuated hanmigamae. Therefore, it makes the most sense if tori stands straight forward.

Sodedori

Sodedori is when uke grips tori's jacket by the end of the sleeve. It is closely related to *gyakuhanmi katatedori*, so if uke stands with the left foot forward, then tori has the right foot forward, and vice versa. Of course, uke should stand with the same foot forward as the hand doing the grip.

Do the grip mainly with the little finger, and with the same angle of the hand as in katatedori.

The grip should be done in the spirit of being an initial attack, with a readiness to continue with other attack forms.

It is not a very interesting attack form, except for its lack of physical contact body to body. This makes it a little more difficult for tori to gain control of uke, than in katatedori. Usually, this grip is mostly trained in the double form, *ryosodedori*. Still, it's not one of the major attack forms in aikido. Many dojos almost never practice it.

Ryosodedori

Ryosodedori is when uke grips tori's jacket by the end of both the sleeves. It is closely related to *ryotedori* (and to *sodedori*, of course), so if uke stands with the left foot forward, then tori has the right foot forward, and vice versa.

Grip mainly with the little finger, and with the same angle of the hand as in katatedori. Stand straight toward tori, not in a hanmigamae angle, for better control. If tori stands in too much of a hanmigamae angle, this grip is awkward to apply for uke. Therefore, it's best if both face each other straight on.

The grips should be done in the spirit of being an initial attack, with a readiness to continue with other attack forms – like kicking, pushing, or pulling.

It is not a very interesting attack form, except for its lack of physical contact body to body. This makes it a little more difficult for tori to gain control of uke, than in for example ryotedori. Usually, this grip is trained in the double form, ryosodedori, and not in the single version sodedori. Still, it's not one of the major attack forms in aikido.

Ryohijidori

Ryohijidori is when uke grips both of tori's elbows. It is closely related to *ryotedori* and *ryosodedori*. The stance is the same: if uke stands with the left foot forward, then tori has the right foot forward, and vice versa.

Grab around the elbows. For better control, face tori straight on, not in a *hanmigamae* angle. Also, if tori initially stands in too much of a hanmigamae angle, this grip is awkward to apply for uke. Therefore, it's best if both face each other straight on.

The grips should be applied in the spirit of blocking tori from attacking. It's not easy to control somebody's elbows, which are strong even on persons who are not very muscular.

This grip is mostly trained in the double form, ryohijidori, and not in the single version *hijidori*. That is why only the former is treated here. It is not one of the major attack forms in aikido, and those few times it is practiced, it is usually from behind, *ushiro*, which is described later in this book.

Just as *sodedori* is good for training aikido on a distanced kind of attack, without body contact, hijidori is good for ex-

Aikido

periencing close contact, with much less room for tori to move the arms than in most other attack forms. Many aikido techniques become sort of shortened when done against it.

Yokomenuchi

Yokomenuchi is when uke strikes at tori's temple with the side of the hand. The attack is related to *sho-menuchi*, but here the stance has a gyakuhanmi relation: if uke has the left foot forward, then tori has the right foot forward, and vice versa. Uke should have the same foot forward as the hand that strikes, for maximum power in the strike.

Like shomenuchi, this is really a sword attack, but done with an unarmed hand for safety reasons. The hand in this form is called *tegatana* (hand sword). The angle of the strike is not horizontal, but diagonal. In *kendo*, Japanese fencing, the difference between shomen and yokomen is not much at all.

Apply your hand the same way as in shomenuchi, and remember to stiffen it, especially at the side of the hand. Make sure to swing your whole arm in the strike, not just the forearm. Keep your arm in the unbendable arm form. Let your other hand follow a bit behind, to resemble the two-handed sword grip, but not as much as in shomenuchi.

Don't allow yourself too much of a *hanmi* angle to your stance, although it's tempting as the attack is a bit from the side. But you lose a lot of power and sharpness in the strike if you do not face tori straight on.

There is an unarmed attack in karatedo, similar to yoko-menuchi. It is done with *shuto*, a hand side strike, in a circular horizontal movement. Usually, this technique is not the one intended in aikido, but the diagonal sword cut. Of course, it is possible to train both.

When you do the karatedo shuto technique, you should allow your elbow to extend to your side, so that you can swing the forearm forcefully in the horizontal strike. But when you do the sword form, it is not correct to open yourself up with your arm out to the side. It has no purpose in the sword strike, so it only opens your guard to counterattacks.

Unfortunately, this opening at the elbow is done by so many aikidoists that they allow tori's defense technique to adapt to it. Aikido techniques modified in this way run the risk of being practically impossible, if a correct sword style yokomenuchi is done. For example, an aikido defense that starts by blocking the striking

arm at the side of uke's body is possible on the karatedo shuto technique, but not on the sword attack, when done correctly. Uke's arm is just not moving enough to the side.

Practicing defense against yokomenuchi is a good way of understanding just about any attack from the side – whether armed or unarmed, a hand strike or a kick. For example, the techniques against yokomenuchi should also work against *yokotsuki*, explained below. It is also important that techniques that work on shomenuchi do so against yokomenuchi as well, since there is not enough time to perceive which of the two attacks is coming.

Katadori menuchi

Katadori menuchi is a combination of two attacks: *katadori* and *shomenuchi*. Uke grabs tori by the shoulder, and immediately follows up with a shomenuchi strike. Since the initial attack is katadori, the relation between uke and tori is that of gyakuhanmi: if one has the left foot forward, then the other has the right foot forward, and vice versa. For how to apply the katadori grip and the shomenuchi strike, see the texts about those, above.

In most aikido dojos, the students are taught that tori should wait for the second attack, the shomenuchi. I am not really fond of that, since a basic principle of aikido should be to act on what comes first. It is far better for tori to treat the attack as a katadori, since that is what comes first. A correct initial *taisabaki* evasion should result in the shomen missing its target, anyway.

Still, waiting for the shomenuchi instead of acting immediately on katadori, is good training for tori. Primarily, it teaches how to avoid a strike even when caught in a grip. That needs to be practiced, as well.

I would recommend students to practice both timings, and not always just one. The early timing at the katadori attack is the superior one, and should be practiced exactly for that reason. The late timing at the shomenuchi should be practiced for the sake of learning how to get out of such a situation.

The different timings can be compared to the training forms *gotai* and *jutai*.

Gotai, hard body, is to practice aikido techniques from a static position, for example when uke's grip has already been applied. *Jutai*, soft body, is done in movement, the aikido technique commencing right before uke's grip has been applied. So, acting at the katadori is like jutai training, and waiting for the shomenuchi is like gotai. Both training forms are important, the former for learning timing and flow, the latter for learning how to get out of strong holds, and how to handle some resistance.

But that is of little concern to uke, of course. Uke should just make sure to do the attack so that there is no pause between the katadori grip and the shomenuchi strike. The katadori grip is intended to keep tori from avoiding the shomenuchi strike, so that's the attitude with which uke should perform this attack.

It is also possible to follow up the katadori grip with other strikes, such as *yokomenuchi, jodantsuki*, a knee to the belly, et cetera. Such combinations are not basic attack forms in aikido, but it is interesting to try them now and then.

Kata katatedori

Kata katatedori is a combination of two attacks: *katadori* and *katatedori*. Uke grabs tori by the wrist and the shoulder, either simultaneously or in very quick succession. Usually this is done with the same foot forward as the hand that applies the katadori grip, since it is otherwise difficult to reach the shoulder, and uke's stance is less stable. Because of this, the relation between uke and  tori is gyakuhanmi – that is, if one has the left foot forward, the other has the right foot forward, and vice versa.

For how to apply the katadori and the katatedori grip respectively, see the above texts about those. Notice that the katatedori grip is like aihanmi, but the stance is like gyakuhanmi.

This is a rare attack form in aikido. It is not very practical if uke is alone in doing it, since both arms will be locked, while tori has one arm free. In *futaridori* (two attackers), though, it is an excellent way to keep control of tori's both arms. That's when it gets really interesting to find aikido solutions.

The challenge for tori in kata katatedori lies in the complexity caused by the two grips. Many aikido techniques, even the most basic ones, have to be modified considerably to work against this attack. To begin with, tori has to decide whether to do the technique on the katadori or the katatedori arm. The wrong choice may lead to a dead end, so that tori gets as stuck as in a maze. Kata katatedori should be practiced more than it normally is, so that aikido students can study the techniques in this complicated setting.

Yokotsuki

Yokotsuki is a horizontal fist strike to the side of the head or the chin. It is rarely used in Japanese martial arts, but a real classic in boxing, where it is called a swing or a hook.

To do it with any power, you need to extend your arm to the side, and use a horizontal body rotation in the strike. If you want to learn it properly, study how it is done in boxing, because it needs that dynamic way of using the body, instead of the usually quite straight way the body moves in for example karatedo.

Pay attention to the angle of your wrist, so that the force of the strike is in line with your forearm. Otherwise the wrist might bend at impact, and may even get hurt. Just like with regular *tsuki*, the knuckles of the index finger and the ring finger are the ones to hit the target first.

The movement most similar to yokotsuki in the Japanese martial arts, is the swing style *uchi* strike done with *jo*, the stick, especially when its angle is close to horizontal. Apart from that, the strike has some similarity to *yokomenuchi*.

This type of attack is so rare, and different from the norm in budo, that the defender is usually surprised by it, and finds it difficult to avoid. Tori needs to adapt his or her *irimi* entrance, to make it safe against yokotsuki. It is also important to consider the heavy body weight behind such a strike, when continuing with an aikido technique on it. On the other hand, what works against yokotsuki should work against just about any attack from the side – including yoko-menuchi.

Mawashigeri

Mawashigeri is the roundhouse kick in karatedo. It is not as easy to learn as the straight *maegeri*, presented above. Still, with a reasonable amount of training, you should be able to do it on *chudan* level, belly height. But the *jodan* level mawashigeri, to the head, demands some agility that is time consuming to achieve, so in most aikido dojos it is not exercised.

Just like with maegeri, you need to raise your knee before you do the actual kick. You keep a better guard if you have a straight posture and angle when you raise the knee, and turn sideways only for the kick. Your knee points forward the whole time.

There are two possibilities for what surface you kick with – either the base of your toes (the ball), like in maegeri, or the upper side of your foot. The latter is the most common, but for chudan kicks to the waist, the former is more effective.

You can kick with your front leg or with the back one. For basic training the latter is to prefer, since it includes the advancing step you should need to reach tori. Your arms should follow: the same arm as leg is moved forward. This gives a better guard and balance.

Because mawashigeri is an attack from the side, I sort it

with the gyakuhanmi relation attacks. Still, it may as well start with an aihanmi relation between uke and tori. The kick belongs to the gyakuhanmi group mainly because of how tori needs to relate to it.

Of course, it is interesting for tori to experience the mawashigeri attack, practice how to meet it and how to do the aikido techniques in such a situation. Still, considering the many things needed to be exercised in aikido, mawashigeri might not be important enough for the time it takes to learn properly. As for the defense against it, *yokotsuki* and even *yokomenuchi* are decent substitutes, since they are dealt with similarly.

Aikido

Ushiro relation

後

Morotedori
Ushiro ryotedori
Ushiro ryokatadori
Kubishime
Eridori
Kakaedori
Ushiro ryosodedori
Ushiro ryohijidori

Ushiro relation
The ushiro relation is when the attacker comes from behind, or starts from the front but moves to the rear of the defender. In training, it is usually done so that uke starts in front of tori, and steps behind him or her – often after initially grabbing one wrist or shoulder, as explained below.

Morotedori
Morotedori (also called *katate ryote-dori*) is when uke grabs one of tori's arms with both of his or her hands. Normally, it is not regarded as an ushiro form, since many aikidoists simply grab the arm in front of tori – but I see little meaning in such an attack form. It locks both of uke's arms, but only one of tori's, and still uke stands right in the way of tori. Not wise.

I prefer when uke grabs the arm and immediately steps behind tori, holding up tori's arm to block him or her from spinning around. There, uke is reasonably protected from tori countermeasures. Also, with such a grip on tori's arm, uke can quite easily block tori from spinning around.

If the attack starts from the front, uke begins by grabbing tori's wrist in *aihanmi katatedori* style (the right hand grabs tori's right wrist, or the left hand grabs tori's left wrist). Immediately after that – preferably in a flowing movement – uke steps behind tori and applies the other hand's grip right above the first hand.

Uke's two hands should not grip tori's arm with a distance between them, although that might seem to be an effective way of blocking some  aikido techniques. But it is an inferior grip, generally speaking, since it gives less control of tori's arm movement.

The morotedori grip is similar to that used in the *yonkyo* aikido technique. Actually, uke can increase the control of tori by applying yonkyo pressure, if tori tries to turn toward uke. If tori instead tries to spin around to uke's rear, uke can stop it by moving tori's arm in that direction. If tori tries to kick, uke can block it by pressing the arm down. Correctly applied, this is quite a good control grip.

Observe that because of the position of tori's arm and uke's hands on it, the aikido techniques need to be done a bit differently from if uke grabs the arm straight in front of tori.

Just like with any grip, it is important for uke to focus on the little fingers, and to have the sword grip style upward angle on the hands. Read more about the grip on aihanmi katatedori, above.

To maximize power and control, it is also important for uke to have the hands and feet in a correct position: When tori's right arm is grabbed, uke's left hand should have the upper grip (the closest to tori's elbow), and uke's left foot should be in front. If tori's left arm is grabbed, then uke's right hand should grab above the left, and uke's right foot should be in front. This gives the best stability, and stops tori from easily lowering his or her elbow.

Finally, uke should keep his or her elbows tight to the

body, and not extended. Again, this increases the power of the grip significantly. It also protects against kicks.

Correctly applied, morotedori is quite difficult for tori to counter. Also, several of the aikido techniques need some modification for them to work, which is very good for tori to experience and explore.

Ushiro ryotedori

Ushiro ryotedori is when uke grabs both of tori's wrists from behind. Normally, this position is reached by uke first grabbing one of the wrists from the front, in *aihanmi* style (the right hand grabs tori's right wrist, or the left hand grabs tori's left wrist), and then quickly stepping around to tori's back to grab the other wrist.

Because of the way uke moves to get behind tori, and the way tori moves in evasive *taisabaki* steps while uke proceeds, they will end up with opposite feet forward: If uke has the left foot forward, tori has the right foot forward, and vice versa.

For example, if uke starts by grabbing tori's right wrist, tori stands with the right foot forward. Uke will round tori's right side and grab the left wrist from behind, ending with the left foot forward. It seems complicated, but it's the most natural way of doing it. Uke will want to have the best balance for grabbing the second wrist, which is accomplished by the foot on that side being forward.

Regarding how the hands should do their grips, see *aihanmi katatedori* above.

When uke has grabbed the first wrist, it is important to lower it, before going behind tori. Otherwise tori could easily hit uke with the elbow, when uke passes by tori's side.

In aikido, ushiro is never trained *katatedori*, gripping just one wrist, since that is a very impractical attack form. The idea with most ushiro attacks is that uke controls tori from behind and tries to stop tori from turning around. That is virtually impossible with just a katatedori grip.

For uke at all to try ushiro ryotedori, starting from facing tori, tori's other arm must be reasonably available from the back. That is, tori has to let that arm drop to the side, or even hold it a bit backward, for uke at all to try ushiro ryotedori. If tori holds both hands in front, for example in some kind of guard position, uke would be much more likely to grab ryotedori from the front (*mae*), than to try for ushiro.

For tori, the interesting thing about ushiro ryotedori is the firm control uke has on both of tori's arms. Even with moderate strength in the grips, tori will find it difficult to get out of them. The arms are much weaker behind the body than in front of it. You need some trick, like those in the aikido curriculum, to free yourself.

Ushiro ryokatadori

Ushiro ryokatadori is when uke grabs both of tori's shoulders from behind. Similar to *ushiro ryotedori* above, this position is usually reached by uke first grabbing one of the shoulders from the front, and then stepping to tori's back to grab the other.

The second shoulder is easier to find and grab from behind than the wrist, so here it is of little concern how tori is positioned beforehand. For details about the katadori shoulder grip, see *katadori* above. To achieve the most control of tori, remember to grab the sides of the shoulders, and not the tops of them. To avoid getting your fingers damaged, don't get them snared into tori's jacket.

In aikido there is no ushiro training of katadori, gripping just one of the shoulders from behind, since that is quite impractical, at least compared to gripping both. The natural thing is to go for both shoulders or none of them.

The challenge of this attack form is for tori to get control of uke's body – and to get to it at all, which is not easy.

Kubishime

Kubishime is when uke locks tori's neck from behind, which is almost always done together with a *katatedori* grip on tori's wrist. Therefore the attack is also called *katatedori kubishime*. Since it is from behind, the full name of the attack would be ushiro katatedori kubishime, but the ushiro is taken for granted, since kubishime is not done from the front. The classical wrestling front side neck lock is not practiced in basic aikido, which is a pity. It is probably excluded because tori's arms are not properly controlled in it.

When applying kubishime, uke usually starts from the front with gripping one of tori's wrists, *aihanmi* style (right hand grabs right wrist, or left hand grabs left wrist). Then, uke moves behind tori and applies the neck lock.

The neck lock can be done in a number of ways, for example with or without grabbing tori's collar. Uke will have the best balance and stability if the same side foot is forward as the arm applying the neck lock. Also, uke should not be positioned right behind tori, but a little to the wrist grip side. This way, it is more difficult for tori to reach uke with the free hand.

The reason for the katatedori grip is to lock one of tori's arms, so that tori has greater difficulty to counter the neck lock. Uke should pull tori back with the neck lock, so that tori stands in a backward arch. For maximum stability in the katatedori grip, uke should press tori's wrist to the hip.

For tori, kubishime is particularly good to experience because of its extremely close and tight uke position. Also, any neck lock tends to create some panic in those unfamiliar with it.

Kubishime is a neck lock, and not a strangulation. Actually, no strangulation attack – either from the front or from the rear – is included in aikido. I don't know why. Maybe they are regarded as too easy to counter, which is far from always true, or maybe they are seen as too rude attack forms for aikido, which also makes little sense.

Anyway, a singlehanded strangulation from the front can be compared to *munedori*, and handled similarly by tori. From the back it is similar to *eridori*. A two-handed frontal strangulation can be dealt with much like *ryokatadori*, or again like munedori. From the back the two-handed strangulation is best dealt with as eridori, although some modifications are needed.

Eridori

Eridori is when uke grabs tori's collar from behind. Therefore, the complete name would be ushiro eridori, but the ushiro is taken for granted. To reach the back of the collar from the front, uke would have to be in a judo type clinch with tori – and then, surely, there must have been a preceding attack form for tori to act upon.

A grip on the actual front of the collar would be *munedori*, described above.

Since the back of the collar is

so difficult to reach from the front, even if uke starts by moving around toward tori's back, this might as well be trained by uke initially standing behind tori, when grabbing the collar.

For the best stability, uke should stand with the same hand and foot forward. Normally, but not necessarily, tori and uke will stand with the same foot forward. As with any grip, most of the power should be in the little finger, and the elbow should be pointing downward.

Eridori is not a tremendously practical attack technique, but it is trained in aikido because it creates some complications for tori in doing the usual aikido techniques. This is due to the difficulty for tori to get to uke's arm.

Kakaedori

Kakaedori is when uke grabs tori's body like a hug, but from behind. The complete name would be *ushiro kakaedori*, but the technique is rarely trained from the front in aikido, so the ushiro is taken for granted. In wrestling, grabbing the opponent from the front is common, so it could be interesting to practice also in aikido. I guess that it is not done because normally in aikido, one should act before uke gets near enough to apply the grip – and for kakaedori uke needs to get very near.

This also means that the attack is regarded as a surprise from behind. So, it might as well be trained with uke initially standing behind tori, instead of uke beginning in front of tori and then moving behind him or her.

There are two ways of doing kakaedori. The most com-

Jaroslav Sip getting out of Jan Hermansson's kakaedori, at a seminar in Plzen,Czech Republic. Photo by Antonín Knízek.

mon one in aikido is where uke grabs around tori's arms, too. The other one is when uke grabs inside tori's arms – embracing the body only. I have never heard that they have separate names. The first one is taken for granted. I recommend aikido students to practice both forms. They lead to quite different solutions for the aikido techniques.

For the best stability, uke should stand with one foot back, not with the feet together. The hands clasp in front of tori, at about solar plexus height, pressing tori tightly toward uke. The clasp of hands can be done in many different ways, such as one hand grabbing the other by the hand or the wrist, or the fingers of both hands hooking. It makes little difference.

When doing the first form of kakaedori, where tori's arms are also caught, apply it approximately at elbow height. If higher, it is too easy for tori to sneak under the grip. If lower, it is too easy to get the arms up, escaping the grip. That has no significance with the second form of kakaedori, where tori's arms are not caught. You may want to apply this kakaedori on tori's chest, not lower. Otherwise tori can turn around rather easily.

Kakaedori is a challenge for tori, since uke gets so close, and uke's arms are particularly difficult to control. A strong kakaedori is not easy to escape.

Ushiro ryosodedori

Ushiro ryosodedori is when uke grabs both tori's sleeves from behind. Similarly to *ushiro ryotedori*, it usually starts from the front, so that uke grabs one of the sleeves and then moves behind tori for the other one. Also the steps are done in the same way, as well as the foot positions of uke and tori.

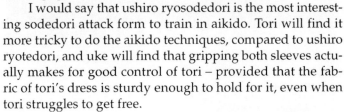

This attack form is not done much in aikido, although it belongs to the curriculum. As mentioned about *sodedori* above, it is mainly of interest because of its lack of contact between uke and tori, compared to for example ryotedori.

In ushiro, sodedori is never practiced with a grip on just one sleeve, since that is an impractical attack form. It is always both sleeves. Regarding the actual sleeve grip, see the text about sodedori, above.

I would say that ushiro ryosodedori is the most interesting sodedori attack form to train in aikido. Tori will find it more tricky to do the aikido techniques, compared to ushiro ryotedori, and uke will find that gripping both sleeves actually makes for good control of tori – provided that the fabric of tori's dress is sturdy enough to hold for it, even when tori struggles to get free.

Ushiro ryohijidori

Ushiro ryohijidori is when uke grabs both tori's elbows from behind. Similar to *ushiro ryotedori*, it usually starts from the front, so that uke grabs one of the elbows and then moves behind tori for the other one. Also the steps are done in the same way, as well as the foot positions of uke and tori.

This attack form is rarely done in aikido, probably just because *hijidori* from the front is also rare. In ushiro, hijidori is never practiced with a grip on just one elbow, since that is an impractical attack form. It is always both elbows. Grab the elbows firmly. It's not easy to hold on to elbows, since they are strong also on less muscular people.

The ushiro form of this attack is more interesting to train than its frontside version, since the grab makes more sense from behind. Also, it is interesting for tori to make sort of narrow versions of the ushiro ryotedori techniques, because uke is closer and grabs higher on tori's arms.

Strikes from behind

Strikes from behind are normally not practiced in aikido, since it is not realistic to escape them if the attacker is not observed beforehand. Nonetheless, some of the budo legends, such as aikido's founder Morihei Ueshiba, were reputed to develop a sensitivity that made it possible for them to escape attacks from behind. They could feel them coming, as if equipped with sort of a mental radar.

It may seem like purely mythical stuff, but I will have to insist that serious martial arts training leads to quite sharpened senses, so something akin to that ability might emerge.

Anyway, it goes beyond the scope of this book, so I leave it be, except for one remark: That sensitivity can only be exercised properly if the attacks are indeed sincere, focused, and forceful.

WEAPONS

短刀 刀

本 劍

杖

Tanto Bokken Jo

Tanto 短刀

Tanto (also called *tanken*) is the knife used by uke in the practice of *tantodori*, defense against knife attacks. For safety reasons, a wooden knife is used. It happens in some aikido demonstrations and dan examinations that a real steel knife is used instead, or an unsharpened replica – but that is not very recommendable.

Even with a wooden tanto, be cautious in training. Wood is hard, and the tip of the tanto is particularly dangerous.

Whatever material, the knife is modeled after the traditional Japanese knife, which is sharpened on one side only, and has a slight curve similar to that on *katana*, the Japanese sword.

In the knife attacks of aikido, the tanto is grabbed firmly with one hand. During the training, uke shifts hands, so that tori can practice defense on the left as well as the right side.

Both the straight grip, with the blade on the thumb side, and the reversed one with the blade on the little finger side, are used. The former is for most *tsuki* and *shomenuchi* attacks, the latter for *yokomenuchi*.

In some dojos, though, the straight grip is used for all attacks. I would not recommend that. The Japanese knife fits better for reverse grip use, actually also in shomenuchi attacks. Only with tsuki strikes, the straight grip makes the most sense.

You should grip with the most power in your little finger, just like with a sword – or any grip in aikido. When your grip is the straight one, where the blade is on the thumb side, the normal position is with the edge downward. But try it also with the edge up, to make tori careful with any blocking movements.

The relation in stances between tori and uke in tantodori is usually *aihanmi*, i.e. both have the same foot forward. It is not that important, though, so you should definitely try the *gyakuhanmi* relation too. When facing armed attacks, tori should not be distracted by foot positions.

Tsuki

The most practical grip for *tsuki* is with the edge to the side. In that angle, the blade is the most dangerous, causing the most damage if the strike succeeds. If you hold the tanto in your right hand, the edge should be to the right, and in your left hand to the left. This is because you don't want to aim the edge toward yourself, since you might start a strike from the side of your body.

There are two targets for tsuki: *chudan*, the belly (at solar plexus), and *jodan*, at the neck. There is less distance between them than one might think, so the angle of the striking arm is almost the same. At least, the difference is too small for tori to need any particular adjustment of the aikido techniques.

The strike is done pretty much like unarmed tsuki with the fist. It should accelerate, and you need to pay attention to the angle of your wrist, so that it is strong, which is with the knife in line with your forearm. Step forward with the leg on the same side as your striking arm, for the best stability, balance, and reach.

In tsuki attacks, it is also possible with the reversed position, *gyakutsuki*, where the opposite leg advances. But that is rare.

At the start, uke and tori usually have the *aihanmi* relation, i.e. with the same foot forward. But the reversed, *gyakuhanmi*, should also be tried.

Shomenuchi

In *shomenuchi*, you always step forward with the leg on the same side as the hand that holds the knife. Also in *yokomenuchi*. The reverse would be awkward, weak, and unbalanced.

Shomenuchi is a downward cutting movement aiming for tori's forehead. It is usually made with the straight grip where the blade is on the thumb side, although that really makes little sense. With the reverse grip, there is much more power to the attack. The reason for the least practical grip is probably its similarity to sword technique. Try both.

With the reverse grip, it is most common to hold the knife with the edge outward, away from the wrist. In old times, though, the edge was held inward, in the direction of the wrist, so that the back of the blade could be used to block swords. That's the reason for the *gokyo* way of tori grabbing uke's wrist from above instead of below, to avoid being cut by the knife.

Aikido teachers have their own preferences on this point, so you might as well try both ways of holding the knife.

The shomenuchi strike is done the same way as in the unarmed form described above. Keep your arm in the extended unbendable arm curve. The other hand can follow slightly behind, but it is not altogether necessary, since this is not a sword attack. It is still good to have it there, as a kind of guard.

At the start, uke and tori usually have the *aihanmi* relation, i.e. with the same foot forward, just as in unarmed shomenuchi.

Yokomenuchi

Yokomenuchi aims for the side of the head. It is also possible – although unorthodox – to aim for the side of the neck. The angle is slightly diagonal, but really not much different from the vertical direction of *shomenuchi*. You don't need that much of an angle to strike at the temple or the side of the neck.

The strike is done in quite the same way as barehanded yokomenuchi, described above. Avoid to open your elbow to the side more than absolutely necessary. Accelerate in the strike, and step forward with the leg on the same side as that of the hand holding the knife. Keep your arm extended in the unbendable arm form.

At the start, uke and tori usually have the *gyakuhanmi* relation, i.e. with opposite feet forward, just as in unarmed yokomenuchi.

There is also a reversed yokomen strike, *gyaku yokomenuchi*, where you strike from the left with your right arm, or vice versa. It is not often practiced in aikido although it is a quite a common knife attack. You should try it. This is one of the few attacks that tori needs to block in order to do some aikido techniques.

Other strikes

Of course, the knife can be moved in so many more ways than the above, but there is not room in the aikido curriculum for all. Still, the basic attack forms used in aikido should be enough to get reasonably acquainted with knife attacks, and learn how to defend oneself against them.

Tantodori targets

Chudantsuki

Jodantsuki

Shomenuchi – reversed

Shomenuchi – straight

Yokomenuchi

Gyaku yokomenuchi

Tachidori targets

Chudantsuki

Jodantsuki

Shomenuchi

Yokomenuchi

Kesagiri

Kote

Yokogiri

Aikido

Bokken

Bokken (also called *bokuto*) is the wooden sword used for safety reasons in the aikido practice of *tachidori*, defense against sword. It is also used in *aikiken* exercises, where both uke and tori have a sword.

The Japanese swords arts have a long history, so they have grown to be quite complex. To the *samurai*, the warrior aristocracy, the sword was the most cherished weapon, regarded with reverence.

There was also magnificent craftsmanship in the making of it, producing a blade with both beauty and extreme sharpness. It was quite costly, too.

It has many names in the Japanese language, the most common being *to*, *ken*, *tachi*, and *katana*. In aikido, these names are used without much distinction between them.

I have written a book about the sword art fundamentals and principles, *Aikibatto: Sword Exercises for Aikido Students*. In the present book, though, I focus on the sword basics that apply to uke's use of the bokken in tachidori training.

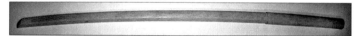

There are many different types of bokken, the wooden sword. Aikido practitioners favor those with shapes similar to the katana, which are about 100 centimeters long (in Japanese measurements: 3 *shaku* and 3 *sun*) and slightly curved. In some aikido schools, though, a thicker and straight one is preferred. Its material is usually oak. You should get one that is solid and dense, like those of quality oak, and with a balance that you appreciate.

Although the sword is wooden, your skills will benefit if you handle it as much as possible as you would a sharp steel sword (*shinken*). Grip it the same way, move it the same way, and treat it with similar respect.

Everything about the sword arts is utterly sophisticated and advanced. Just cutting properly is a lifetime pursuit. So is gripping it: The two-handed grip should be applied with a soft strength, and the hands turned upward-inward, somewhat like squeezing the hilt.

Most of the power in the grip is in the little fingers. If you grab firmly with them, and forget about the other fingers, the balance of force between the fingers will automatically be the correct one: approximately 50% in the little fingers, 30% in the ring fingers, and 20% in the middle fingers. The index finger and thumb use almost no power at all in the sword grip.

The palms of your hands should have tight contact with the sword, so that there is no air between the wood and your skin. When your grip gets good, you can feel your energy streaming through the whole of the bokken, all the way to the tip of it, and then further on to what you aim for.

When you hold and move the sword, your shoulders should be relaxed. Your power comes from your center, *tanden*, and your arms are extended in the unbendable arm form.

Kamae

The sword guard most commonly used in aikido is *chudankamae*, where you hold the sword right in front of your center. Also in the Japanese sword arts, it is the most favored and trusted guard. But there are others, such as *jodankamae*, over your head, *hasso*, over your shoulder, and *migiwaki*, by your right side.

In tachidori training, almost only the chudankamae is used, but the other guards should also be tried now and

Chudankamae, the middle guard, with bokken. Seminar in Lucenec, Slovakia. Photo by Martin Svihla.

then. They result in different *maai*, the initial distance between uke and tori, and in different timing.

These four kamae with the sword are closely related, which you can see when moving from one to the other.

Chudankamae

If you start in *chudankamae*, you have your right foot a full step forward. Keep your body weight evenly balanced between the feet, for optimal freedom of movement. The feet should not be that far apart to the sides. They should not be on a straight line, but just a few inches to either side of it, since you need all your force to go for-ward or backward, but rarely to the sides. Also, the narrow stance of the feet tends to make you a smaller target for an opponent's sword, which is what the sword arts usually take for granted that you are up against.

Your feet should not point forward, but slightly to one side. With your right leg forward, as in chudankamae, both your feet should point slightly to the left. This gives more power to your legs for sudden movements forward or backward. Of course, if you stand with your left leg forward, your feet should point slightly to the right.

You hold your bokken in front of your center, your arms extended in the unbendable arm fashion. The sword is not horizontal, but angled slightly upward. If you imagine an extended curve from your bokken, it should hit the left eye of tori. It doesn't have to be that exact, but with some training you will automatically be rather precise in this aim.

You should face tori straight on. That means the line of your shoulders should be at a 90° angle from the direction to tori. It doesn't have to be exact, but you should not allow too much of a *hanmigamae* angle. That comes later.

Don't stare tori in the eyes, if you don't feel vastly superior. Eyes can get caught – and tricked, too. The best is to

Kamae with bokken

Moving from chudankamae, through jodankamae, hasso, and migiwaki.

look in the direction of tori's chest, but not in a staring way. Make your gaze open, so that you will react also to the surroundings. You just fix your eyes at tori's chest, because that is the best spot for seeing any body movement of tori. Tori should use the same technique, by the way, and most of all avoid staring at the bokken.

Jodankamae

Now, when you shift to *jodankamae*, you raise your sword without bending your arms – i.e. pushing forward more than pulling up. At the same time you either advance with your left foot, or step back with your right foot, depending on the circumstances. When your bokken lands in the correct jodan position over your head,  you stand with your right foot about half a step behind the left one – not more. It is a high guard, so it should have a high stance.

Because you now have your left foot in front of the right one, your feet should point slightly to the right.

Your body has turned slightly, from a position facing tori straight on, to a somewhat angled position, sort of halfway to a *hanmigamae*, the stance so popular in aikido, where one side of the body is more forward than the other. Compared to the direction to tori, the line of your shoulders should be at about 60°. It doesn't have to be that precise, just keep in mind not to exaggerate this angle.

Hold the bokken in an angle that makes its hilt point at tori's face, preferably the left eye, but that is neither very important nor easy. The bokken is not held horizontally, but sloping slightly.

Make sure that you hold your arms so that you can see tori between them. Don't let your elbows point to the sides. That will make your strike weak and unsharp. It is better that you have a high position with the sword, than that you

Aikido

bend your arms too much – especially when you are learning this.

The sword cut is actually done in the same way as you lifted the sword to jodan – although the other way, and much faster. So, if you learn to lift the sword to jodankamae really fast, you are actually also learning how to cut with it.

Other aspects of jodankame are the same as for *chudankamae*, described above.

Hasso

Hasso (or *hassogamae*) is the shoulder guard. You reach it from *jodankamae* by bringing it down toward your shoulder in a curved trajectory. Hasso should be done on the right side, since a left side hasso would be very weak an awkward.

At the same time as you lower your bokken toward your right shoulder, your right foot

slides backward a little less than half a step, so that you end with your right foot about three quarters of a step behind the left one. It is still a rather high position, although not as much so as jodankamae.

Since your right foot has moved slightly more backward, your feet should now point slightly more to the right – especially the right foot, if that is comfortable to you. But don't let the foot turn a full 90° angle from the direction to tori. That is far too much, and makes you lose some of your forward focus and power.

Also, you increase the angle of your body into a full *hanmigamae* position, where your right side is distinctly backward, compared to your left side. Your shoulders should not be in line with the direction to tori, but at about a 45° angle to it. It doesn't have to be precise, but try to avoid overdoing the hanmi. You must still be focused forward, and not at all to the side.

The angle of the sword should be more upward than in

jodankamae. Not completely vertical, not at all. That would make your sword grip awkward, and a quick cut would get very imprecise. The sword should still lean backward, but no more than about 45° from vertical. In the sword arts, there are many different ways of doing hasso, and many angles to hold the sword. So don't worry about it, but find an angle that you are comfortable with, in spite of what I said above.

The edge of the sword is still pointing forward, toward tori, not at all to the side.

In hasso, your arms need to bend more than in the previous guards, but you don't need to point to the sides with your elbows. Let the upper arms rest on your chest, and hold the sword some five or six inches above your shoulder – the height that is comfortable to you.

When you strike, you move the sword back the way it came, through jodankamae and all the way back to chudankamae. You move your body accordingly.

Migiwaki

If you lower the sword even more to your right side from *hasso*, you end up in *migiwaki*, the right side guard. In this guard, you hold the sword either horizontally, or slightly sloping.

Your body moves when you lower the sword. Your right foot slides backward until it is one full step, or even a little more than that, behind the left foot. Your body turns until the line of your shoulders are almost in the direction of tori – but not completely, because then you would lose power and focus forward. Let's say 20°, but don't take that literally. Your feet turn slightly more to the right, but not all the way to 90° from the direction to tori.

In migiwaki you stand in a low position, with your feet far apart, like a cat preparing to pounce. The edge of the sword points to the right. Your left arm is extended in the unbendable arm fashion, while the right arm has to bend slightly more.

This guard is rarely used in aikido, maybe because it seems to be the slowest starting point for striking forward. That is not true. Correctly done, a strike from this position can be very fast indeed. When you do it, you move backward through the guard positions mentioned above – to *hasso*, *jodankamae*, and cut down to *chudankamae*. It can be done in an instant.

Strikes

The basic striking techniques used in aikido's tachidori are *chudangiri*, where you cut vertically down to chudan level, *shomenuchi*, where you stop at the neck, *yokomenuchi*, where you cut the head diagonally, *chudantsuki*, where you thrust at the belly, and *jodantsuki*, where you thrust at the neck or head.

The sword arts contain additional techniques, of course. The most important of those are *kesagiri*, where you cut the body diagonally, and *do* or *yokogiri*, where you cut the body horizontally at belly height. They should also be tried in tachidori, since they are valued techniques in the sword arts, and because they change the attacking angle and therefore also tori's defense.

Chudangiri

Chudangiri is the very basic and primary technique in the sword arts. It is a vertical cut from *jodan* to *chudan* level, i.e. from over the head down to the *chudankamae* guard position with the sword in front of one's center. Since this is the very most important of the sword techniques, it is practiced much more than other techniques with the sword. It is also by far the most commonly used one in tachidori.

Normally it is done in two steps: You start in chudankamae, step forward with your left foot and simultaneously lift your bokken to *jodankamae*, then take a step with your right foot and do the chudangiri cut. In the advanced way,

you actually lift your sword at the beginning of the second step, since you want to open your guard for as short a time as possible, and you strike right before the end of that same step.

The distance between you and tori should be such that you reach with the two steps described above. Tori should never allow you to start so near that you could reach with a *tsuki* thrust without taking a step forward, or the distance where you can just slide forward on your front foot to reach with tsuki. Many aikido students are sloppy with this, allowing the attacker to stand so near that the sword tip almost touches them. Of course, tori must not trust that the attack will be *kiri*, the cut, when tsuki makes more sense.

Stopping the sword at chudan level may seem difficult, but there is a trick to it. Don't try to do it by muscular force only. That will make your shoulders tense, and still the sword will dip at the end, instead of stopping precisely where it should. Instead, make sure to extend both your arms in the unbendable arm fashion, and secure your two-handed grip on the sword. That way, the sword will stop where it should, because your arms will not allow it to go beyond that point.

Another way of describing it is that you don't stop the sword by keeping the tip of the sword from going any deeper, but by letting your left hand and arm hold down the sword hilt. When it can't go up, the tip can't go down.

Still, the technique of stopping the sword at the right level takes some time to learn. Before you can do it, you

Aikido

probably make your shoulders tense in every strike. To avoid this when learning to cut in a relaxed way, don't stop the sword at chudan level, but let it continue down to *gedan*, the lowest level. Only to the extent that you are able to relax when you do the cut, should you allow yourself to practice stopping the sword at chudan level.

At the start, uke and tori usually have the *aihanmi* relation, i.e. with the same foot forward. But the reversed, *gyakuhanmi*, usually works just as well.

Shomenuchi

Shomenuchi, the vertical strike to the head, is done quite the same as *chudangiri* above, except for stopping the cut at neck level. This stop is accomplished by extending your arms forcefully forward – not so that they become completely straight, but so that the strike is halted. You should still keep the unbendable arm form.

The steps and the timing are the same as in chudangiri, but you don't need to get down as low, since you aim for a higher target.

An alternative way of doing shomenuchi is from *jodankamae*, where you hold the bokken over your head and you stand with your right foot half a step behind the left one. With this guard, you can be closer to tori to begin with, since the sword is not in front of you. To reach with your strike, you should only need to take a step forward with your right foot, and strike at the end of the step.

This is a quick attack, so tori should be apt to it. Be careful when practicing this type of shomenuchi.

At the start, uke and tori usually have the *aihanmi* relation, i.e. with the same foot forward, just as in unarmed shomenuchi. That is true also when uke stands in jodankamae.

Yokomenuchi

Yokomenuchi is the diagonal strike to the head. You do it much the same as *shomenuchi* above, except for the direction of the actual strike.

Observe that there is not that much difference in the angle of yokomenuchi, compared to shomenuchi. The former is done with an angle just around 30° from vertical, absolutely no more than 45°. You can accomplish it with a slight turn of your hands, so that you don't have to change the position of the arms much at all. You keep them almost the same as if you were doing shomenuchi.

Don't adjust the sword for yokomen during the strike. That makes your cut imprecise and much less powerful. Make the adjustment right before you strike. Not long before, because tori will see this and be warned, but at the very moment when you are about to strike, which is at the end of your last step.

You can easily do yokomenuchi from *chudankamae* and *jodankamae*, just like shomenuchi. You can also do it from *hasso*, in which case you start from approximately the same distance as you have in jodankamae – or slightly more, because you are able to make a longer leap forward from this position than you are from jodankamae.

It is also quite possible and reasonable, although not common, to make yokomenuchi from the *migiwaki* guard. Here you should have a starting position even more far from tori than in hasso, since you can leap even further from this low and powerful stance. But you should not stand as far from tori as in chudankamae, since you must reach tori with just one step, albeit a particularly long one.

When striking yokomen from migiwaki, you can adjust the angle of the sword and your grip earlier than at hasso and jodankamae, since tori can't really see what strike you prepare, in the angle that you hold your body.

At the start, uke and tori usually have the *gyakuhanmi* relation, i.e. with opposite feet forward, just as in unarmed yokomenuchi. If uke doesn't start from *chudankamae*, though, the *aihanmi* relation is often to prefer.

Chudantsuki

Chudantsuki is the basic thrust technique in the sword arts. Its aim is tori's belly, more precisely solar plexus or right below it. The best guard to start from is *chudankamae*, of course. Then you need do little more than thrust the sword forward. So, it is also the quickest.

Your distance should be the same as when you do *chudangiri*, described above, for the simple reason that tori should not allow you to stand any nearer. So you still have to take two steps, making the thrust at the end of the second step.

Tsuki with the sword is not a straight line thrust, but a curve similar to half the trajectory of a spear throw. It starts with an upward movement, becoming almost horizontal at the end. This is mainly to make the very point of the sword tip go first. That way, even very hard objects can be penetrated. It is also practical against somebody with a sword held in chudankamae, since that curve sneaks over the opponent's guard.

You can hold the sword with the edge pointing down all through the movement, or you can tilt the sword so that the edge is to the side at the end of the thrust. This is common in the sword arts, since a thrust this way easier slips through body armor – and the ribs, if tsuki is done that high (for example when aiming for the heart). When you make your thrust with the edge sideways, it should point to the other side than your front leg. If your final step is with your right leg, the edge should point to the left, and vice versa. This increases the power and stability of the thrust.

Don't make the thrust with excessive bodily power. That only risks getting you needlessly out of balance. The Japanese blade is sharp enough, and certainly its tip, so the thrust will work even if it is done rather softly.

It is also important not to aim too far with the thrust, so that you lean forward and thereby lose most of your balance. Also, this would make you extend your arms too much, whereby they become easy targets. Instead, step up close before making the thrust, so that the length of it only has to correspond to the width of tori's body. Some ten to fifteen inches is usually enough.

At the start, uke and tori usually have the *aihanmi* relation, i.e. with the same foot forward, just as in unarmed tsuki. Still, the reversed, *gyakuhanmi*, should be tried sometimes.

Jodantsuki

There is really just one difference between *jodantsuki*, the high thrust, and *chudantsuki* described above: the aim of the technique. Jodantsuki aims for the neck.

This alters the trajectory of the thrust, giving it a sharper upward curve to begin with, and a slight upward angle also at the end of it.

Apart from that, everything about the technique is the same as for chudantsuki.

Kesagiri

The most common sword technique in samurai days was one rarely done in aikido's tachidori: *kesagiri*, the diagonal body cut. It is named after the suspenders worn by Zen monks, *kesa*, which are diagonal. An example of slightly bizarre samurai humor.

The angle of the cut is not that very far from vertical, just about 30° or so, definitely not as much as 45°. It was supposed to enter at the base of the neck, and either not exit at all, or do so on belly height at the opposite side of the body.

Because of the armor worn by the samurai, this was the most practical cut in the battlefield. A vertical cut was usually stopped by the helmet.

The angle of the cut makes it similar to *yokomenuchi*, described above, but kesagiri goes on at least to *chudan* level. In basic training of it, stopping the sword at chudan level is to prefer, but traditionally it was also done all the way to *gedan*. Especially in the battlefield, where stopping the sword would only be tiresome in the long run.

You can do kesagiri from any *kamae*, but it is particularly practical from *hasso*, because there the sword is already at the correct angle. You just move forward with your right foot and strike without passing over *jodankamae*. Quite naturally, the cut will have the kesagiri angle.

Also from *migiwaki*, kesagiri is smooth and practical.

You can also do kesagiri from left to right, but that is

more difficult. Your sword grip and arm positions get a little awkward on the left side. Still, it's doable and should be exercised.

The most difficult thing with kesagiri is to keep the cut straight. In every cut, the blade has to move exactly in line with the edge, or it will not cut that well. In kesagiri it easily happens that the cut turns into a curve instead of a straight line. This takes diligent training to cure. Check yourself by doing the cut slowly, and watch where the edge is pointing throughout the whole movement.

At the start, uke and tori usually have the *gyakuhanmi* relation, i.e. with opposite feet forward, just as in yokomenuchi. If uke starts from another guard than *chudankame*, though, the *aihanmi* relation is often to prefer.

Yokogiri

Yokogiri (also called *do*) is the horizontal cut. It doesn't have to be completely horizontal. Any sideways cut to the body below the arms is called *yokogiri* or *do*. The latter is simply the name of the chest guard worn in *kendo*, Japanese fencing.

For tachidori purposes, the horizontal cut is the best, because it differs the most from the other sword cuts practiced.

The trick with it is to adjust one's sword grip and arm positions, in order to do the strike with enough power and precision. If you move the sword horizontally, the edge must point exactly the same way all through, and that's not easy. It's not even easy to stick to a horizontal direction. Most people who try it do a curved kind of cut that dips in the middle.

To get power enough in the cut, and to keep it horizontal, go into a low stance, and use a body turn. It is a bit like baseball.

For easy practice of it, use *migiwaki*, the right side guard. Take a big step forward with your right foot, turn your body to the left and swing the sword simultaneously. You can also do it from the left side, *hidariwaki*, where you stand with your left foot back and hold your sword by your left side.

Aikido

Take a big step forward with your left foot, turn your body to the right and swing the sword to the right simultaneously.

Yokogiri is what makes the side guard kind of scary for tori, because a cut from this angle can only be avoided by a *taisabaki* movement to the other side. Therefore, tori should really do only that kind of taisabaki when faced with migi-waki or hidariwaki. Even with a taisabaki evasion at the correct side of uke, defense against yokogiri is not easy.

On the other hand, if tori also has a sword, defending against yokogiri is much easier – a simple parry that can quickly be followed up by a strike that uke has little chance to avoid. That is probably why the side guards are not that commonly used in the sword arts. In aikido, though, that is no reason for not trying it – frequently, for tori to learn how to avoid it.

At the start, uke and tori usually have the *aihanmi* relation, i.e. with the same foot forward, because that makes yokogiri a reasonable choice for uke. The only exception is if uke starts from *chudankame*, in which case the *gyakuhanmi* reversed relation works equally fine.

Jodantsuki

Yokomenuchi

Chudantsuki

Kote

Gedantsuki

Gedanuchi

Jo 杖

The jo needs to be handled quite differently from the sword. This is obvious when compared with the real steel sword, but easy to forget when practicing only with the wooden bokken. That is the case with many aikido students, who therefore tend to make their jo movements more similar to sword ones than they should be.

Contrary to the bokken, the jo is the real thing. What you see is what you get – a wooden stick. It cannot cut, and it cannot pierce. Simply speaking, you hit with it. That needs more power in the strikes than what is necessary with a steel blade. Also, you need to put weight behind your techniques for them to have any effect. Try to remember that when you use the jo: apply firm grips with both hands, and use your whole body in the strikes.

Your body movements will approach those of a boxer, or a baseball player with the bat. Dynamic body turns bring power to the techniques.

Pay attention to your grips on the jo. They need to be quite firm. Otherwise the jo may slip out of your hands when you strike something. Also, without firm grips you have little chance of making the strikes drive through. At the moment of impact, your grips should be rock hard.

The little fingers are the most important ones, also with the jo. But because of the additional force needed, you must tighten all your fingers hard at the strikes.

Again to ascertain the force of the strikes, you should have such an angle on your wrists that your forearms are in line with the strikes, supporting and adding strength to them.

The hand is weaker than the arm, so your grips should be such that it's like the jo is directly connected to the arms. Don't hold the jo just with your fingers, but tighten them so that it has maximum contact with the palms of your hands.

Of course, you have to loosen the grip when your hand slides on the jo, but avoid doing that with both hands at once. There should always be at least one hand with a steady grip on the jo.

Whatever strike you make, be sure to do it with your whole arm, and with your body behind it. All through the jo practice, try to focus on making the strikes so that you feel that there is power behind them. Otherwise, the jo techniques have little meaning.

There are many different techniques with the jo, of course, but for tori in *jodori*, defense against jo attacks, there is basically one aspect that matters the most: how the hand is turned in uke's front grip of the jo. It can be like a sword grip, with the little finger the closest to uke, or reversed, so that the thumb is the closest to uke. That makes all the difference in the world for tori in most aikido techniques.

There are some one-handed strikes as well, but they are neither important enough to consider as much, nor strong enough to cause any similar problem for tori. The challenge for tori is to make aikido techniques while uke keeps a two-handed grip on the jo, unwilling to let go of it. Many techniques – even quite basic ones – get difficult because of this.

As for the strikes with the jo, there are again many different ones possible, but in aikido it makes sense to focus of a few, which are the most important ones.

There is *tsuki*, the thrust, which can be done on three levels: *jodan*, *chudan*, and *gedan* (high, middle, and low). The high one aims for the head or neck, the middle one for solar plexus, and the low one for the knee. For tori it doesn't matter much which one is done, since the aikido technique response is pretty much the same for all three.

What matters is the position of uke's front hand. When it is like a sword grip, it's called *chokutsuki*, and the reversed is called *kaeshitsuki* (or *gyakutsuki*). These two are described below.

The *uchi* strikes, where the jo is swung toward the target, also have three levels. Jodan is against the head, chudan is against the wrist, and gedan against the knee.

Jodan is done *yokomen*, to the side of the head, because there is little meaning in striking the top of the head with a

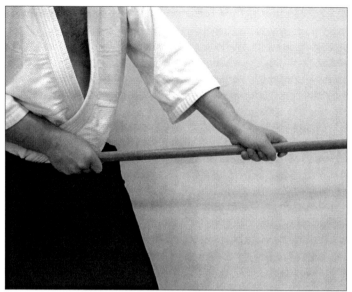

Chokutsuki grip.

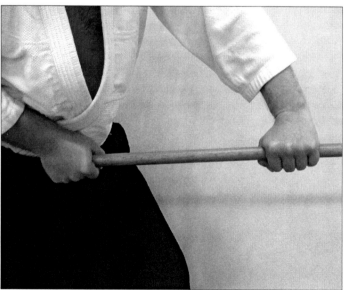

Kaeshitsuki grip.

Attacks 107

jo. Chudan against the wrist is only done against an opponent who is armed, traditionally with a sword. On an unarmed opponent, the wrist strike is quite meaningless. The gedan strike to the knee is either to make the knee bend and thereby cause the opponent to lose balance, or to dislocate the kneecap, whereby that leg is no longer possible to walk on.

The uchi strikes can all be done with either of the two front hand grips described above, but the reversed grip usually makes them more powerful. Still, both should be tried.

When tori is beginning to learn doing aikido techniques against jo attacks, it is fine to settle for tsuki attacks only – but both chokutsuki and kaeshitsuki, since they lead to sometimes quite different solutions. There is no point in immediately trying also against all the uchi strikes. The aikido solutions are very similar, whether there is a tsuki thrust or an uchi strike.

There are two main traditions in the aikido practice with the jo. In the mostly spread one, the jo is initially held vertically on the ground, right in front of the forward foot, sort of like a walking stick. In the other tradition, which is more closely linked to the martial art *jodo*, the jo is held by the side with one hand on the middle of it and the other hand on the front end.

I recommend aikido students to get familiar with both these traditions, just for the sake of being able to adapt on seminars and such.

Chokutsuki

Chokutsuki is the thrust where your front hand grip on the jo is with the little finger the closest to you, like a sword grip.

If you start from the position with the jo vertically on the ground, you hold it about one third down with the same side hand as the foot that is forward. The jo is placed right in front of that foot, which is no more than half a step from your back foot.

You should stand in *hanmi-gamae*, with the body a bit sideways – but not too much, or you will not have enough power forward. Your shoulders should be at about a 45° angle from the direction to tori. Don't worry too much about it, but find the angle comfortable for you.

Lift the lower end of the jo backward by turning your wrist, and catch it at its end with your other hand. Let it slide until your front hand is by the other end of the jo, so that you hold it from end to end in a horizontal position.

At the same time, slide forward with your front foot. The back foot follows just a little, because you want to end up in a lower posture, for the sake of stability. This kind of step is called *tsugiashi*. You don't need to advance more than that, because of the long reach of the jo. More pre-

cisely, your back foot follows at the moment of your thrust, to give additional power to that movement.

By the end of the step, thrust your jo forward by pulling your back hand all the way to your center. Your forearm will actually hit your belly, which is just good – it means that your thrust ends with a strong body support. You let the jo slide in the forward hand, which tightens firmly at the end of the thrust.

Because of your initial *hanmi* stance, you will advance slightly sideways, not straight on. This is a kind of *taisabaki* evasion, traditionally used not to get struck by the opponent's sword.

You should be able to do this technique right-sided as well as left-sided.

If you have the *jodo* initial position, with the jo held by your side, your stance is the same as for the previous form. Your back hand holds the middle of the jo, and your front hand holds the front end, traditionally with the tips of the index finger and the middle finger covering the end of the jo.

The angle of the jo is such that it points toward tori's left eye – but it doesn't have to be that exact. The idea with this angle, except for its advantages as a guard position, is that tori will not see the full length of the jo, and might forget to take proper precautions.

You slide forward with your front foot, the same way you would from the other guard position. At the same time,

Aikido

your back hand slides backward on the jo until it reaches the end of it. Thereby, you grip the full length of the jo.

By the end of your forward step, thrust by pulling your back hand forward, the same way you do with the previous chokutsuki. At the same moment, slide a little bit forward with your back foot, to add power to the thrust – and to get the foot out of line with tori.

Kaeshitsuki

Kaeshitsuki (also called *gyakutsuki*) is with the reversed forward hand grip on the jo.

If you start with the jo vertically on the ground, with one hand about a third down from the top, as described in *chokutsuki* above, your first movement is to grab the top of the jo reversed, with your free hand. Then you pull the jo backward, sliding through your first hand grip until it reaches the other end of the jo. When you hold it at both ends, the jo is horizontal.

At the same time, advance with your front foot, just like in chokutsuki. At the end of the step, you strike by thrusting the jo forward with your back hand, stopping when that hand is right in front of your center.

Apart from the different hand movements, this kaeshitsuki is done like chokutsuki from the same starting position.

If you start with the jo by your side, you need to move quite differently from how you do chokutsuki from the same starting position.

First, turn your front hand, holding the top of the jo, so that it grabs in the reversed way. Then pull the jo backward in a circular movement, toward the other side of your body. You need to twist your body to the same side in order to do it. You also need to turn the front foot to that side. The jo slides through the other hand, until reaching that end of the jo. At this point, the jo is horizontal.

Take a full step with you back foot. Strike at the end of the step, by thrusting the jo forward with the hand holding its backward end, until your hand is right in front of your center. Observe that the front hand will now have a reverse grip, because of how you have moved the jo.

This movement might be unfamiliar to some aikido students, but it is a classical *jodo* tsuki, more commonly used than chokutsuki in that martial art. Make sure to practice it, for a better understanding of how to use the jo.

Yokomenuchi

The *jodanuchi* (high level strike) with the jo is *yokomenuchi*, a strike to the side of the head – more precisely the temple. You have the most power if you hit with the very end of the jo, because of its edge.

Also, make the movement circular, so that all its force is directed to the target at impact – not slightly elliptic, as you would with the corresponding sword cut.

Your forward arm should be in such a position that it gives maximum support to the strike, i.e. behind the jo in the direction of the strike. Your backward arm is not right in front of your center, but a bit higher up, at about lower chest height.

If you start with the jo vertically on the ground, yoko-menuchi is simple to get to.

Grab the top of the jo with you free hand in a reversed grip, i.e. with your thumb down. Slide forward with your front foot. At the end of the step, strike by moving the jo in a big circle, so that it hits from above, at an angle slightly more diagonal than you would with a sword, say 45° or so from vertical. Not a full 90°, because that would be a weaker strike.

There is another way of doing yokomenuchi from the same starting position, more similar to the sword technique. Here you strike

the other side of the head. Grab the top of the jo with a straight grip by your free hand, and pull the jo up, sliding through the other hand's grip, until it reaches the lower end of the jo. You need to make the pulling movement in a backward curve, to reach and to prepare for the strike.

Take a full step forward with your back leg, and strike at the end of the step by swinging the jo diagonally forward, sliding your upper hand downward. Make sure not to allow the striking move of the jo to go out to the side, but right ahead to the target. Again, the angle of the strike should be around 45°.

If you start from holding the jo by your side, reverse the grip at the top of the jo. Then, take a full step forward with you back foot, and strike in the same circular way as described in the first yokomenuchi form above. Because you take a full step, instead of just sliding forward with your front foot, you need to start further away from tori.

Another way of doing yokomenuchi from the same

Aikido

Attacks 115

starting position strikes the other side of the head. Here, you don't reverse the front hand grip, but just pull the jo up, sliding it through your lower hand grip until it reaches the lower end of the jo. You need to pull the jo in a backward curve in order to reach, and to prepare for the strike.

At the same time as you pull the jo, slide forward with your front foot. Strike at the end of the step, by letting your upper hand slide down the jo, without bending your arm. Make sure to have the 45° angle, and to support the strike with your front arm behind the jo. Your back hand ends at about lower chest height.

So, above you have four ways of doing yokomenuchi with the jo. Try them all. The most common in aikido *jodori* training is the first one – and the third, for those who prefer the *jodo* starting position. Notice that the first and third strikes end with the reversed forward hand position, whereas the second and fourth strikes end with the straight forward hand position – something very important for tori to be aware of, when doing the aikido technique.

Kote

The *chudanuchi* (middle level strike) with the jo is *kote*, a strike to the wrist. It is mostly used against an opponent armed with a sword, standing with it in *chudankamae*. Against an unarmed opponent it makes little sense. Therefore, it is rare in aikido's *jodori*, defense against the jo. It is still good to know, which is why it is included here.

If you start with the jo vertically of the floor, grip it re-

Aikido

versed by the top with your free hand, slide forward with your front foot, and strike with a big circular movement of the jo. It is quite the same as the first yokomenuchi above, although the target is different.

For proper power, it is very important that you strike from above, and not from the side. So, the striking move ends vertically. Also, make sure to use your whole body, lowering it distinctly at the end of the strike. You should have enough force downward to be able to stop the opponent from lifting the arm.

The second way of the strike described in yokomenuchi above, with a straight forward hand grip, is not practical for kote. It does not have sufficient power on *chudan* level, and you will have trouble stopping the opponent from lifting the arm.

If you start with the jo by your side, you reverse the front hand grip, take a full step forward with your back foot, and strike with a big circle. It is quite the same as the third

yokomenuchi described above, except for the target of the strike, and the additional downward power needed.

The fourth yokomenuchi strike described above is not meaningful in kote, because it is not strong enough on *chudan* level.

Gedanuchi

The *gedanuchi* strike, the lowest of the three *uchi*, aims for the knee. It can be done in all the four forms described for *yokomenuchi* above, and in much the same way. The target is different, of course, and therefore also how to use the body.

You need to pull through the strike by a forceful body turn. For that power to work in line with your strike, you must have a low position and also lean your body slightly forward. The gedanuchi should strike horizontally for maximum effect. Adjust your body so that you can do this comfortably and powerfully.

In the first of the four forms described for yokomenuchi above, you need a small adjustment when you aim for the knee. In the beginning, your free hand should apply the straight grip instead of the reversed one. It is more powerful for a strike on knee height. Try both, and you will immediately discover why. With a reversed grip, your hand position gets quite awkward in the strike.

The same is true for the third type of strike, starting with the jo by your side. Don't reverse your front hand grip.

In the second and fourth types of strikes you don't need to consider this. But remember that in gedanuchi they are not as powerful as the first and third types are. Also, it is quite difficult to make them horizontal, which would be the best. Therefore, don't bother to do them as much as the other ones. But try them out.

Aikido

TABLES

Techniques and Attacks

Attacks

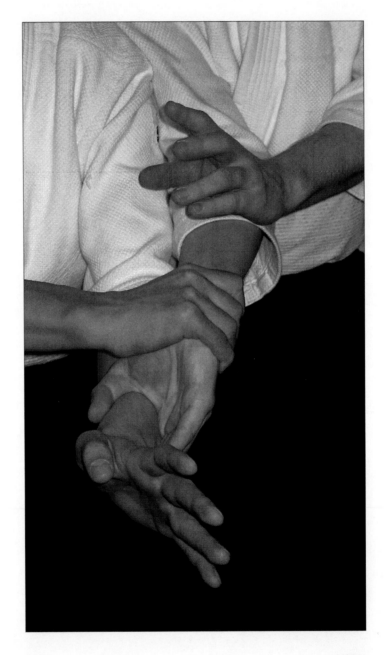

Techniques and attacks in aikido

Tachiwaza mae (*standing, attacks from the front*)
Tachiwaza ushiro (*standing, attacks from the rear*)
Suwariwaza (*tori and uke sitting*)
Hanmi handachiwaza (*tori sitting, uke standing*)
Tantodori (*defense against knife*)
Tachidori (*defense against sword*)
Jodori (*defense against staff*)
Kaeshiwaza (*counter techniques*)
Henkawaza (*changed techniques*)
Renzokuwaza (*consecutive techniques*)

General principles

The basics listed here are not all the executable techniques of aikido, but almost. Aikido contains a number of throwing and pinning techniques, which vary somewhat, depending on the attack. All of them cannot be considered basic, but most of them should indeed be included in the aikido curriculum.

A good system of basic techniques should be compatible with other aikido schools. In regard to how the techniques are done, as well as to what techniques are included, a system of basics should be such that the aikido student is able to adapt to the training in another dojo than his or her own.

This does not mean that all aikido schools should be identical, or even similar in how they do the techniques. But good basics should be possible to adapt to other solutions, and not alienate the students.

Basic techniques should be reasonable to perform. Too complicated solutions are not basic. Some techniques are basic against certain attack forms, but not against other ones, where they are very awkward or difficult to do. Furthermore, any basic technique should in itself be reasonably straightforward.

Attack forms that are not reasonably feasible are not

Present aikido doshu, Moriteru Ueshiba, showing hanmi handachiwaza ryotedori at a demonstration in Stockholm. Photo by Magnus Hartmann.

included in the basics. Some attacks, or combinations of attacks, are so difficult or awkward for the attacker that they are quite unlikely, therefore not to be included in a basic system.

Also other techniques than these basics of the following tables may be executable and trained. It is important to train more than the basics, to progress well in aikido. Also variations and complicated non-basics should be tried with some frequency. Otherwise the aikido in a dojo risks shrinking to something less than can be expected.

Good technical solutions should work from *gotai*, a static position where uke has applied the grip, as well as from *jutai*, in movement, where uke has not completely grabbed hold of tori. In the comments below, gotai solutions are implied, where they are applicable – i.e. all the grips but none of the strikes. Jutai solutions are much simpler, but also much less of a challenge. Both need to be practiced.

In the tables, techniques that are underlined have additional information and video clips on my aikido website:

www.stenudd.com/aikido

Aikido

Tori principles

取

Always start with *taisabaki*, the evasive movement! It is not aikido if not started by avoiding the oncoming attack – even if the attack is a mild or slow one.

Blocking the attack should not be necessary. To block the oncoming force is not really aikido, which should avoid confrontation. Sometimes blocking is practical, but if it is necessary, then the technique needs modification.

Techniques should be functional. An aikido technique should be possible to do in a way that avoids the attack, as well as controls the attacker.

There should be similar solution for *gotai*, from a static position, and *jutai*, in movement. If a basic technique that works in movement needs to be significantly changed when done from a static start, it should be modified – and vice versa.

Basic training should be done with low postures. The balance and control of low stances is essential to have as a standard demand for basic techniques.

Forces should be united (*aiki*). In aikido techniques, the forces of the attacker and the defender should be joined, and not work against each other.

The need for *atemi*, strike, should be limited. The aikido techniques should be possible to do with few or no atemi, which otherwise tend to be 'an easy way out'.

Tori's starting position should be such that uke's attack is reasonable. The target that uke is supposed to aim for must be easily reached – not hidden or blocked or otherwise awkward for uke.

Tori's starting position should not be such that only one aikido technique is appropriate. It is no good if tori is positioned ideally for one aikido technique, but awkwardly for other techniques. Tori should have an initial stance making him or her able to do many different techniques.

Tori should control the situation all through the technique. From the start to the finish, whether it is a pinning or a throw, tori should be in charge and remain aware.

Ryotedori at a beginners class in the author's former dojo Brandbergen, Sweden. Photo by Magnus Burman.

Aikido

The fundamentals (such as center, *ki*, posture, etc.) should always be stressed in training the basic techniques. The techniques are mere expressions of the fundamentals, and do not work well without them.

Uke principles

It is part of the aikido basics to learn correct attacks. Uke is obliged to attack with as much sincerity as applied to the aikido techniques when being tori. Otherwise, aikido cannot be learned properly.

Attacks should normally be done with low postures. The balance and control of low stances is essential as a standard for most basic attack techniques, in order to do them correctly.

Uke should not intentionally resist the technique. There is no point in resisting a particular technique, thereby being additionally vulnerable to other techniques. Also, resisting somebody who is trying to learn a technique is counter-productive.

Uke should have a continued spirit of attack, through the technique. Uke should remain in an attacker mind all through, keeping the aim at tori.

Uke should not change direction of the attack, during the technique. Uke's initial aim toward tori should remain all through, unless the exercise specifies differently.

The fundamentals (such as center, *ki*, posture, etc.) should always be stressed in training the attacks. The attack techniques are mere expressions of the fundamentals, and do not work well without them.

Katamewaza – pinning techniques

Ikkyo

Nikyo

Sankyo

Yonkyo

Gokyo

Aikido

Hijikime osae / Rokkyo

Kaiten osae

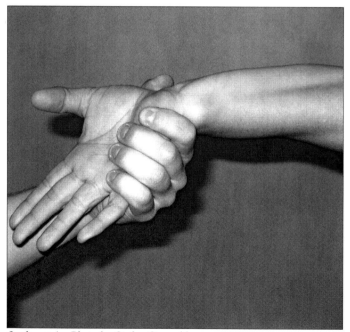

Sankyo grip. Photo by Stefan Stenudd.

Attacks 127

Nagewaza – throwing techniques

Kokyuho

Kokyunage

Iriminage

Shihonage

Kotegaeshi

Tenchinage

Kaitennage

Koshinage

Udekimenage

Jujigarami

Ushiro kiriotoshi

Aikinage

Aiki otoshi

Aikido

TACHIWAZA - MAE

bas = basic   adv = advanced/difficult   - = not basic/possible

	aihanmi katate dori	gyaku hanmi katate dori	ryote dori	morote dori	kata dori	ryo kata dori	mune dori	ryo sode dori	ryo hiji dori	shomen uchi	yokomen uchi	chudan tsuki	jodan tsuki	mae geri	mawashi geri	kata dori men uchi
KATAMEWAZA (pinning) *in order of importance*																
ikkyo omote/ura	bas	bas	bas	bas	bas	bas	bas	bas	bas	bas	bas	bas	bas	bas	bas	bas
nikyo omote/ura	bas	bas	bas	bas	bas	bas	bas	bas	bas	bas	bas	bas	bas	bas	bas	bas
sankyo omote/ura	bas	bas	bas	adv	bas	bas	bas	bas	bas	bas	bas	bas	bas	bas	bas	bas
yonkyo omote/ura	bas	bas	bas	adv	bas	bas	bas	bas	bas	bas	bas	bas	bas	bas	bas	bas
gokyo omote/ura	-	-	-	-	-	-	-	-	-	bas	bas	bas	bas	-	-	-
hijikime osae omote/ura	adv	bas	bas	-	bas	adv	bas	bas	-	adv	adv	bas	bas	-	-	bas
kaiten osae omote/ura	adv	adv	adv	-	adv	adv	adv	-	adv	adv	adv	-	-	-	-	adv
NAGEWAZA (throw) *in order of importance*																
kokyuho	bas	bas	bas	bas	bas	bas	bas	bas	bas	bas	bas	bas	bas	bas	-	adv
kokyunage	bas	bas	bas	bas	bas	bas	bas	bas	adv	bas	bas	bas	bas	-	-	adv
iriminage omote/ura	bas	bas	bas	bas	bas	bas	bas	bas	bas	bas	bas	bas	bas	bas	bas	adv
shihonage omote/ura	bas	bas	bas	bas	adv	bas	bas	bas	bas	bas	bas	bas	bas	adv	adv	bas
kotegaeshi omote/ura	bas	bas	bas	adv	adv	adv	adv	adv	bas	bas	bas	bas	bas	adv	adv	adv
tenchinage omote/ura	bas	bas	bas	-	adv	-	adv	-	bas	bas	bas	bas	bas	bas	-	-
kaitennage omote/ura	bas	bas	bas	-	adv	-	-	adv	bas	bas	bas	bas	bas	-	-	-
koshinage	bas	bas	adv	adv	adv	adv	adv	-	adv	bas	bas	adv	adv	-	-	adv
udekimenage	bas	bas	adv	bas	adv	-	adv	adv	adv	bas	bas	bas	bas	-	-	adv
jujigarami	-	-	-	bas	-	-	-	-	-	-	-	-	-	-	-	-
ushiro kiriotoshi	bas	adv	-	-	-	-	-	-	-	adv	adv	bas	bas	bas	adv	-
aikinage	-	-	-	-	bas	-	-	-	-	adv	adv	adv	adv	-	-	-
aiki otoshi	-	-	-	-	-	-	-	-	-	-	-	-	-	-	-	-

Tachiwaza mae 立技前

Tori and uke standing – frontal attacks

Notes on the attacks

Morotedori (also called *katate ryotedori*) is sometimes dealt with as aihanmi katatedori, and sometimes as gyakuhanmi katatedori, depending on which one of uke's arms tori does the technique on.

Morotedori usually counts as *mae*, a frontal attack, although uke should apply the grip almost behind tori, *ushiro*, not to be too open to a strike.

On *katadori* and *ryokatadori* it is usually necessary to break free of the grip, to do the aikido technique.

Tori's entrance on one-handed attacks should be the same as on two-handed, and lead to practically the same execution of the technique.

Sodedori and *hijidori* are usually done as *ryo*, with both hands. In a one-handed grip, they are treated the same.

Tori's entrance on *shomenuchi* should also protect against *yokomenuchi*, and vice versa. The same goes for *jodantsuki/ chudantsuki*, *maegeri/mawashigeri*.

Basic techniques on *shomenate* are done like on *shomenuchi*.

Both *maegeri*, the front kick, and *mawashigeri*, the roundhouse kick, can be done on different heights – usually *chudan* or *jodan* – but it makes little difference to how the aikido technique is done.

Katadori menuchi would be most effective to always handle as *katadori*, commencing before the *shomenuchi* strike, but the most common is to await the shomenuchi and then do the technique on either the shomen or the katadori arm.

Notes on the techniques

IKKYO is the most basic of all aikido techniques, and should be possible to do on any attack. It is also an entrance move for nikyo, sankyo, yonkyo, gokyo and hijikime osae, but it is not always so that they are applicable to all the situations where ikkyo works.

NIKYO is the second most basic pinning technique after ikkyo, and applicable to most but not all attacks – though all in tachiwaza mae.

SANKYO is a bit tricky to do on morotedori, because of uke's hands both being involved in the grip.

YONKYO is a bit tricky to do on morotedori, because of uke's hands both being involved in the grip.

GOKYO differs from ikkyo in two ways: 1) the grip on uke's wrist, 2) the pinning at the end. Gokyo is mainly against armed attacks, such as tantodori. Therefore it is not to be regarded as basic against attacks that cannot be done with a knife.

HIJIKIME OSAE is by some aikido organizations called *rokkyo*, the sixth teaching. It is most often an alternative to nikyo, when uke's arm is straight. Because of its slightly different movement, it becomes more complicated against some attacks. In some aikido dojos, the technique is not regarded as basic at all. Many aikido teachers make no division into *omote* and *ura* of hijikime osae.

KAITEN OSAE is rarely regarded as a basic technique in aikido, which is why it is not marked as basic against any attack in the table. It is like kaitennage, although ending with a pinning instead of a throw. Kaiten osae should be done both *soto* (outer) and *uchi* (inner), where it can be applied. Many aikido teachers make no division into *omote* and *ura* of kaiten osae.

KOKYUHO is by some aikido organizations not regarded as a technique at all, just a basic exercise (usually done in warm-up). That is a pity, since it is a very practical technique, applicable to most situations.

KOKYUNAGE can be done in so many ways. For the basics, a straightforward way of doing it should be used, but advanced students should be able to do several variations of kokyunage against the most basic grip attacks. It is not really functional against kicks, because of the lack of contact and the position uke assumes after a kick.

IRIMINAGE is a very practical technique, easy to do on most attacks. On katadori menuchi it gets a little tricky, though, because of uke's arms being in the way. Many aikido teachers make no division into *omote* and *ura* of iriminage.

SHIHONAGE is easy to do on most, but not all, attacks. Usually, *omote* is easier than *ura*, but on some attacks it is the other way around. Against kicks, shihonage is a bit complicated, because of the extended position of uke's leg after the kick. Also against shoulder grips (katadori and ryokatadori) it is tricky to do, since tori has to break free of the grip first.

KOTEGAESHI is easy to do on most attacks. It gets a little complicated on shoulder grips (katadori and ryokatadori), where tori has to break free of the grip first, and on morotedori because of the two-handed grip. On mawashigeri it is difficult because tori has to enter on the inside of the kick, and on katadori menuchi because tori has to go under uke's katadori arm. Many aikido teachers make no division into *omote* and *ura* of kotegaeshi.

TENCHINAGE is difficult or next to impossible against many attacks, because it needs to extend uke in two separate directions. On katadori and munedori, tori has to break free of the grip to do it. Many aikido teachers make no division into *omote* and *ura* of tenchinage.

KAITENNAGE is difficult against several grip attacks, since it is necessary to break free of the grip first, and then there is a problem of leading uke. Against kicks, it is not very practical at all, because of the position uke assumes after the kick.

Kotegaeshi at a seminar in Pardubice, Czech Republic. Photo by Leos Matousek.

Kaitennage should be done both *soto* (outer) and *uchi* (inner). Many aikido teachers make no division into *omote* and *ura* of kaitennage.

KOSHINAGE is done with different frequency in aikido dojos. Some do it a lot, some very rarely. The technique can be applied to many attacks, and there is a lot of ways to do it. For basic training, a straightforward way should be used. Because of its rarity in many aikido dojos, it is marked as advanced against attacks where koshinage needs to be done in a way less common in aikido, although it may be rather easy to do. On ryosodedori it is particularly difficult because of uke's sleeve grip, which makes is complicated for tori to control uke enough. Against kicks, koshinage is not to recommend.

UDEKIMENAGE is a bit difficult against ryotedori, since tori has to break free of one of the grips beforehand – the same with ryosodedori and ryohijidori. Also against katadori and munedori, tori has to break free of the grip. Udekimenage is not practical against kicks, because of the position uke assumes after the kick.

JUJIGARAMI (also called JUJINAGE) is easy to do against a few attacks, and very difficult against most others, because uke's arms need to be crossed. Since jujigarami is not a very basic technique in aikido, the students need not try to solve complicated situations for it.

USHIRO KIRIOTOSHI is by few aikido teachers regarded as a basic technique at all, wherefore it is not necessary for the students to work that much on it. It is difficult to do when it is tricky to break free of a grip attack, so it is mostly applied on striking attacks.

AIKINAGE is a neat technique against a few attack forms, but hardly a basic technique at all. One needs to be completely free of grips, so it is only to be applied on some striking attacks. The exception is ryokatadori, where aikinage is quite easy in spite of the remaining grips – but maybe in this case, strictly speaking, it should not be regarded as a proper aikinage. Observe that it should not be tried on kicks. It is also questionable on chudan striking attacks and on yokomen.

AIKI OTOSHI is far from basic, and somewhat questionable as an aikido technique, since it involves lifting uke. It is most practical against some ushiro attacks, but never easy to do with conviction. Since it is such a peripheral technique, it is unnecessary for students to practice against other attacks than where the technique is particularly appropriate.

Tachiwaza ushiro　　立技後

Tori and uke standing – attacks to the rear

Notes on the attacks

Techniques in parenthesis are less important or can be excluded in ushiro, because they are awkward to execute or not applicable.

When uke starts in front of tori, on the way to ushiro, tori should make an evasive *taisabaki* step, not to stand in uke's way.

Kubishime as a basic attack is done with *katatedori*, one wrist grabbed.

bas = basic　adv = advanced/difficult　- = not basic/possible

TACHIWAZA - USHIRO	ryote dori	ryo kata dori	ryo kubi shime	kakae dori	eri dori	ryo sode dori	ryo hiji dori
KATAMEWAZA (pinning) *in order of importance*							
ikkyo omote/ura	bas	bas	bas	adv	adv	bas	bas
nikyo omote/ura	bas	bas	bas	adv	adv	bas	bas
sankyo omote/ura	bas	bas	bas	adv	adv	bas	bas
yonkyo omote/ura	bas	bas	bas	adv	adv	bas	bas
(gokyo) omote/ura	-	-	-	-	-	-	-
hijikime osae omote/ura	bas	bas	bas	adv	adv	bas	bas
kaiten osae omote/ura	bas	bas	bas	-	-	adv	adv
NAGEWAZA (throw) *in order of importance*							
kokyuho	bas	bas	adv	bas	adv	bas	bas
kokyunage	bas	bas	adv	bas	adv	bas	bas
iriminage omote/ura	bas	bas	bas	bas	bas	bas	bas
shihonage omote/ura	bas	bas	bas	bas	-	bas	bas
kotegaeshi omote/ura	bas	bas	bas	bas	-	bas	bas
tenchinage omote/ura	-	-	-	-	-	-	-
kaitennage omote/ura	-	-	bas	adv	adv	adv	-
koshinage	bas	-	bas	adv	-	bas	-
udekimenage	-	-	adv	-	-	-	-
jujigarami	bas	adv	adv	adv	-	bas	-
ushiro kiriotoshi	-	-	-	-	-	-	-
aikinage	-	adv	-	-	-	-	-
aiki otoshi	-	-	bas	-	-	-	-

Kakaedori can be done outside or inside tori's arms. In the basic form, the techniques are done with a grip outside tori's arms.

Also strikes can be practiced from behind, but apart from the initial evasive move, they are done the same way as from the front.

Notes on the techniques
For general notes, see the comments on tachiwaza – mae.

IKKYO is easily done on all the attack forms – although slightly trickier on kakaedori and eridori, because these holds are more difficult to get out of. On ryokatadori and eridori it is necessary to break free from the grip.

NIKYO – see what is said about ikkyo above.

SANKYO – see what is said about ikkyo above.

YONKYO – see what is said about ikkyo above.

GOKYO is not basic in ushiro, since there are no strikes.

HIJIKIME OSAE – see what is said about ikkyo above.

KAITEN OSAE is in ushiro only done as uchikaiten, under the arm, since this is the way tori gets out of the grip. On some attacks it is a very impractical or complicated technique to do, therefore far from basic.

KOKYUHO is tricky to do on kubishime, because of the positions of uke's arms, tending to get in the way. It can get tricky also on eridori, if uke's arm is held straight, in which case it is difficult to get close enough to uke for kokyuho.

KOKYUNAGE is reasonably easy to do on all ushiro attack forms.

IRIMINAGE is easy to do on most attacks. On ushiro ryokatadori it can get tricky, if uke holds on to the shoulders. Eridori, too.

Nobuyoshi Tamura, 8 dan Aikikai, in ushiro ryotedori with the author, at a seminar in Malmö, Sweden. Photo by Anders Heinonen.

Attacks 137

SHIHONAGE is easy to do on most attacks. Against ushiro ryokatadori it is quite tricky to do properly, since tori has to break free of the grip first. There is really no reasonable way to do shihonage properly on eridori.

KOTEGAESHI is easy to do on most attacks. It gets a little complicated on ushiro ryokatadori, where tori has to break free of the grip first. There is not really a proper eridori solution for kotegaeshi.

TENCHINAGE is difficult or next to impossible against ushiro attacks, since tori needs to separate uke's arms opposite to their positions in the grips.

KAITENNAGE is difficult or next to impossible against several ushiro attacks, usually because of the need to break free and still lead uke into the technique.

KOSHINAGE is reasonably possible to do against a few ushiro attacks, and very difficult against others. Usually, the need for a certain distance – or closeness – is what creates the problems.

UDEKIMENAGE is easy on two ushiro attacks, complicated on one, and close to impossible on the others. The problem is mostly getting uke's arm in position for the throw.

JUJIGARAMI (also called JUJINAGE) is easy to get to in several ushiro attack forms, where uke's arms cross almost automatically. At eridori, though, tori is not likely to get hold of both uke's arms, and at ushiro ryohijidori it is not realistic to get uke's arms crossed.

USHIRO KIRIOTOSHI is not practical in ushiro, since it demands getting behind uke.

AIKINAGE can be done against ushiro ryokatadori, but not really against any of the other ushiro attacks.

AIKI OTOSHI is neither practical nor simple against any other ushiro attack than kakaedori, where it is instead very suitable.

Suwariwaza　　　　　　　　座技

Tori and uke sitting

Notes on the attacks

Attack forms that are very impractical in suwariwaza are excluded from the table. They are not basic, in some cases hardly possible at all.

Legend: **bas** = basic   **adv** = advanced/difficult   **-** = not basic/possible

SUWARIWAZA	aihanmi katate dori	gyaku hanmi katate dori	ryote dori	kata dori	ryo kata dori	mune dori	shomen uchi	yokomen uchi	jodan tsuki	kata dori men uchi
KATAMEWAZA (pinning) *in order of importance*										
ikkyo omote/ura	bas	bas	bas	bas	bas	bas	bas	bas	bas	bas
nikyo omote/ura	bas	bas	bas	bas	bas	bas	bas	bas	bas	bas
sankyo omote/ura	bas	bas	bas	bas	bas	bas	bas	bas	bas	bas
yonkyo omote/ura	adv	bas	bas	bas	bas	bas	bas	bas	bas	bas
gokyo omote/ura	-	-	-	-	-	-	bas	bas	bas	-
hijikime osae omote/ura	adv	adv	adv	bas	adv	bas	adv	adv	bas	bas
kaiten osae omote/ura	adv	adv	adv	adv	adv	adv	-	-	-	adv
NAGEWAZA (throw) *in order of importance*										
kokyuho	bas	bas	bas	bas	bas	bas	bas	bas	bas	-
kokyunage	adv	adv	adv	adv	adv	adv	bas	-	-	-
iriminage omote/ura	bas	bas	bas	bas	bas	bas	bas	bas	bas	adv
shihonage omote/ura	bas	bas	bas	adv	adv	-	-	bas	bas	adv
kotegaeshi omote/ura	bas	bas	bas	adv	adv	-	bas	bas	bas	-
(tenchinage) omote/ura	-	adv	adv	-	-	-	-	-	adv	-
kaitennage omote/ura	-	bas	adv	-	-	-	-	-	-	-
~~koshinage~~	-	-	-	-	-	-	-	-	-	-
(udekimenage)	-	-	-	-	-	-	-	-	-	-
jujigarami	-	bas	-	-	-	-	-	-	-	-
ushiro kiriotoshi	bas	-	-	-	-	-	adv	adv	adv	-
~~aikinage~~	-	adv	-	-	-	-	-	-	-	-
~~aiki-otoshi~~	-	-	-	-	-	-	-	-	-	-

Techniques in parenthesis are less important or can be excluded in suwariwaza, because they are awkward to execute.

Crossed-out techniques should be excluded from suwariwaza, because they are unsuitable or impossible.

Ushiro on suwariwaza is not basic, although it does exist in several grading systems. It makes more sense if the attack is initiated from the rear – instead of starting by uke moving from the front to the rear, which is too awkward for uke.

Notes on the techniques
For general notes, see the comments on tachiwaza – mae.

IKKYO is easy enough on the attack forms listed.

NIKYO is easy enough on the attack forms listed.

SANKYO is easy enough on the attack forms listed.

YONKYO is easy enough on the attack forms listed.

GOKYO is basic only on the striking attacks. On katadori menuchi it is not meaningful, since it cannot be done on uke's striking arm.

HIJIKIME OSAE is a bit more tricky on some attacks, because of uke's arm needing to be straight.

KAITEN OSAE is in suwariwaza only done as *soto*, outside uke's arm, since it is too difficult for tori to get under uke's arm. On some attacks it is a very impractical or complicated technique to do, therefore far from basic.

KOKYUHO is reasonably easy on all suwariwaza attacks except katadori menuchi, because of the difficulty to move in behind uke.

KOKYUNAGE is not complicated in suwariwaza, but still a bit difficult because of the momentum needed for the throw. That is why it is marked as advanced, when applicable. On striking attacks it is not really practical.

IRIMINAGE is just as basic in suwariwaza as ikkyo is, and trained as much in most dojos. Only in munedori and katadori menuchi does it get a little tricky.

SHIHONAGE is a bit awkward to do in suwariwaza, because of the need of going under uke's arm. Just as in tachiwaza, it is quite difficult to do on katadori and ryokatadori, but here even more so on munedori. Shihonage ura gets extremely difficult in suwariwaza, because of uke being in the way of tori's feet in the turn. So, many teachers do not demand it of their students.

KOTEGAESHI is almost as common to do in suwariwaza as shihonage is. On munedori it is difficult because of the problem for tori to use a flexible enough body movement in suwariwaza. On katadori menuchi the problem is to get under uke's katadori arm. Therefore, they should not be included in the basics.

TENCHINAGE is next to impossible on several attacks in suwariwaza, because of how uke needs to be extended in two different directions, and because uke is unlikely to fall even when this is done. It can be done on more attacks than those marked as advanced here, but that would be very far from basic.

KAITENNAGE should only be done *soto*, outside uke's arm, in suwariwaza – and it is still difficult against any other attack than gyakuhanmi katatedori. Ryotedori is a little trickier than katatedori, since tori has to get free from one of uke's wrist grips.

KOSHINAGE is just not possible in suwariwaza, because of both tori and uke sitting down.

UDEKIMENAGE is possible, sometimes rather easy, to do against several attacks in suwariwaza, but it's not much of a throw, since both are sitting down. Therefore, it should not be included in the basics.

JUJIGARAMI (also called JUJINAGE) is really only applicable on some *ushiro* grips, from the rear. Since these are ex-

Suwariwaza at a seminar in Brno, Czech Republic. Photo by Martin Svihla.

cluded from suwariwaza basics (see the notes on attacks), this throw is excluded as well.

USHIRO KIRIOTOSHI can be done against some attacks in suwariwaza. It takes some swift knee-walking, though, to be done convincingly. On such attacks as katadori and mune-dori, for example, it is not practical because of the need to break free of the grip, and the difficulty in then moving swiftly to uke's rear.

AIKINAGE is not possible in suwariwaza, because both tori and uke are sitting down.

AIKI OTOSHI is not possible in suwariwaza, because both tori and uke are sitting down – not a good starting point for lifting somebody. Anyway, it would really just be practical on some few ushiro attacks, which are not included in these basics (see the notes on attacks).

HANMI HANDACHIWAZA

bas = basic   adv = advanced/difficult   - = not basic/possible

	aihanmi katate dori	gyaku hanmi katate dori	ryote dori	morote dori	kata dori	ryo kata dori	ushiro ryo kata dori	ushiro eri dori	yokomen uchi	shomen uchi	jodan tsuki	mae geri	mawashi geri	kata dori men uchi
KATAMEWAZA (pinning) *in order of importance*														
ikkyo omote/ura	bas	bas	bas	bas	bas	bas	bas	bas	bas	bas	bas	adv	adv	-
nikyo omote/ura	bas	bas	bas	bas	bas	bas	adv	-	bas	bas	bas	adv	adv	-
sankyo omote/ura	bas	bas	bas	adv	adv	adv	adv	-	bas	bas	bas	adv	adv	-
yonkyo omote/ura	bas	bas	bas	adv	adv	adv	adv	-	bas	bas	bas	adv	adv	-
gokyo omote/ura	-	-	-	-	-	-	-	-	bas	bas	bas	-	-	-
(hijikime osae) omote/ura	-	adv	adv	-	adv	-	-	-	bas	-	bas	-	-	adv
kaiten osae omote/ura	-	adv	adv	-	bas	bas	-	-	-	-	bas	-	-	bas
NAGEWAZA (throw) *in order of importance*														
kokyuho	bas	bas	bas	bas	bas	bas	adv	-	bas	bas	bas	adv	-	bas
kokyunage	adv	adv	bas	bas	adv	adv	bas	adv	adv	adv	adv	-	adv	adv
iriminage omote/ura	bas	bas	bas	adv	adv	adv	bas	adv	bas	bas	bas	bas	bas	adv
shihonage omote/ura	bas	bas	bas	bas	adv	adv	adv	-	bas	bas	bas	bas	bas	bas
kotegaeshi omote/ura	bas	bas	bas	adv	adv	adv	adv	-	bas	bas	bas	bas	adv	adv
tenchinage omote/ura	adv	bas	bas	-	adv	-	-	-	adv	adv	adv	-	-	-
kaitennage omote/ura	bas	bas	bas	-	-	-	-	-	adv	adv	-	-	-	-
~~koshinage~~	-	-	-	-	-	-	-	-	-	-	-	-	-	-
(udekimenage)	adv	adv	adv	adv	adv	adv	adv	-	adv	adv	adv	-	-	adv
~~jujigarami~~	-	-	-	-	-	-	-	-	-	-	-	-	-	-
~~ushiro kiriotoshi~~	-	-	-	-	-	-	-	-	-	-	-	-	-	-
(aikinage)	-	-	-	-	-	-	adv	-	adv	adv	adv	-	-	-
~~aiki otoshi~~	-	-	-	-	-	-	-	-	-	-	-	-	-	-

Hanmi handachiwaza 半身半立技

Tori sitting, uke standing

Notes on the attacks

Attack forms that are very impractical in hanmi handachiwaza are excluded from the table. They are not basic, in some cases hardly possible at all.

Techniques in parenthesis are less important or can be excluded in hanmi handachiwaza, because they are awkward to execute.

Crossed-out techniques should be excluded from hanmi handachiwaza, because they are unsuitable or impossible.

Both *aihanmi* and *gyakuhanmi katatedori* are odd attack forms for uke to do in hanmi handachiwaza, if tori does not raise the arm for uke to reach – which is, of course, odd for tori to do. The same is true for *ryotedori*. Still they are all basic.

In hanmi handachiwaza, the attack *morotedori* is done from the side, because it would make little sense from the front, and it is not necessary for uke to go to tori's rear.

Katadori and *ryokatadori* are reasonable attacks for uke to do in hanmi handachiwaza – contrary to the wrist grips – so they should be trained frequently. This is also true for *ushiro ryokatadori*, and to a lesser extent for *ushiro eridori*.

Notes on the techniques

IKKYO needs to start with bringing uke down considerably, which is true for almost all hanmi handachiwaza techniques. In ushiro eridori, tori really needs to stand up to complete the technique, because of the grip in the collar. Against kicks, it can be difficult to get control of uke's wrist, which is hard to reach from sitting down. This is true for all the pinning techniques.

NIKYO can be done on most attacks, with varying difficulty. In ushiro ryokatadori, tori needs to break free of the grip before doing the nikyo pinning. This is true also for ushiro eridori, where it is even more difficult, so it is excluded from the basics.

SANKYO can be done on most attacks, with varying difficulty. It is always complicated on morotedori, because of uke's two-handed grip on tori's wrist. On katadori, ryokatadori and ushiro ryokatadori, it is necessary to break free of uke's grip, before applying the sankyo pinning. This is also true for ushiro eridori, where it is additionally difficult, therefore excluded from the basics.

YONKYO can be done on most attacks, with varying difficulty. It is always complicated on morotedori, because of uke's two-handed grip on tori's wrist. On katadori, ryokatadori and ushiro ryokatadori, it is necessary to break free of uke's grip, before applying the yonkyo pinning. This is also true for ushiro eridori, where it is additionally difficult, therefore excluded from the basics.

GOKYO is only relevant against striking attacks (especially when done with a knife). Therefore, only those attack forms are included in the basics.

HIJIKIME OSAE is not very practical in hanmi handachiwaza, because of tori sitting down. On jodantsuki, though, it is reasonably easy, since uke's arm is straight after the attack. Also on gyakuhanmi katatedori, ryotedori, katadori and ryokatadori, it can be done without too much difficulty.

KAITEN OSAE should be done both *soto* (outer) and *uchi* (inner), when possible. Since it is a peripheral technique, it is only included in the basics for the attacks where it is reasonably easy to do.

KOKYUHO can be done on most attacks, but is generally tricky in hanmi handachiwaza, because of tori's need to bring down uke before the throw. On ushiro eridori it is too difficult to bring uke down, and on mawashigeri too difficult

Hanmi handachiwaza kokyunage at the author's dojo.

Aikido

to enter into a good position for the throw. Therefore, these are not basic.

KOKYUNAGE can be done on most attacks, with varying difficulty. It is very complicated on ushiro eridori, because of uke's position in relation to tori, and on kicks because of uke's extended leg position after the kick, so these are not basic.

IRIMINAGE is quite easy on most attacks, if uke is first brought down properly. Katadori and ryokatadori are a little tricky, because of the difficulty for tori to reach properly. On mawashigeri the problem is bringing uke down. On katadori menuchi it gets quite difficult, because of uke's arms being in the way.

SHIHONAGE *omote* is easy on most attacks. *Ura* is so difficult in hanmi handachiwaza, because of uke's leg being in the way, that many aikido teachers exclude it. In the Hombu Dojo standard form, tori should stand up to complete the throw on ryotedori, ryokatadori and ushiro ryokatadori, in order to be able to bring uke's arms up sufficiently. But that is not necessary if the technique is done well. Standing up can also be allowed on other attacks. On ushiro eridori it is very difficult to do a regular shihonage, so it is not basic.

KOTEGAESHI can be done on most attacks, with varying difficulty. On ushiro eridori it is very comlicated to get to, so it is not basic. On mawashigeri it is tricky to get hold of the wrist, and on katadori menuchi tori needs to do the technique with uke's katadori grip remaining.

TENCHINAGE is difficult on most attacks in hanmi handachiwaza, because of tori sitting down, making it hard to extend uke in two directions. In aihanmi katatedori it is necessary first to break free from uke's wrist grip. It is not practical against kicks.

KAITENNAGE should be done both *soto* (outer) and *uchi* (inner), when possible. It is far from basic on most attack forms in hanmi handachiwaza, because of the difficulty in bringing uke down correctly before the throw. It is not practical against kicks, because of uke's arms being difficult to catch and control in the way needed.

KOSHINAGE is not something to do in hanmi handachiwaza, because of tori sitting down.

UDEKIMENAGE can be done rather easily on some attacks. The difficulty lies in advancing to get enough of a pull in the throw. It is because of this difficulty that the technique can't really be basic in hanmi handachiwaza. It is not practical against kicks, although possible.

JUJIGARAMI (also called JUJINAGE) is very difficult on almost every attack in hanmi handachiwaza, because of tori sitting down, which leads to problems in controlling uke's arms sufficiently. There is no need for including it in the basics.

USHIRO KIRIOTOSHI is not practical at all in hanmi handachiwaza, since it is difficult for tori to reach uke's shoulders.

AIKINAGE is possible to do on some attacks in hanmi handachiwaza, although there is not much of a surprise effect in going down only from a sitting position. When done on ryokatadori and ushiro ryokatadori, it needs to happen before uke's grips are applied.

AIKI OTOSHI is not possible to do in hanmi handachiwaza, because of tori sitting down.

Tantodori　　　　短刀取

Defense against knife

General notes
Crossed-out techniques should be excluded from tantodori, because they are unsuitable or impossible, or lack control of *tanto*, the knife.

In tantodori, the techniques should be practical and as safe as possible. Deviations from this should be clearly pointed out in training.

Tantodori should always be done with good control of the tanto, and end with disarming.

The techniques should also be executable against a double edged tanto.

Returning the tanto to uke should be done with care.

TANTODORI	chudan tsuki	yokomen uchi	shomen uchi	ushiro chudan tsuki
KATAMEWAZA (pinning) *in order of importance*	*bas* = basic　*adv* = advanced/difficult　- =not basic/possible			
ikkyo omote/ura	bas	bas	bas	adv
nikyo omote/ura	bas	bas	bas	adv
sankyo omote/ura	bas	bas	bas	adv
yonkyo omote/ura	-	-	-	-
gokyo omote/ura	bas	bas	bas	adv
~~hijikime-osae omote/ura~~	-	-	-	-
~~kaiten-osae omote/ura~~	-	-	-	-
NAGEWAZA (throw) *in order of importance*	*bas* = basic　*adv* = advanced/difficult　- =not basic/possible			
kokyuho	adv	adv	adv	adv
kokyunage	bas	bas	bas	adv
iriminage omote/ura	bas	bas	bas	adv
shihonage omote/ura	bas	bas	bas	adv
kotegaeshi omote/ura	bas	bas	bas	adv
tenchinage omote/ura	bas	bas	bas	adv
~~kaitennage omote/ura~~	-	-	-	-
koshinage	bas	bas	bas	adv
udekimenage	bas	bas	bas	adv
~~jujigarami~~	-	-	-	-
~~ushiro kiriotoshi~~	-	-	-	-
~~nikimage~~	-	-	-	-
~~aiki-otoshi~~	-	-	-	-

Notes on the attacks

Tori's entrance on *shomenuchi* should also protect against *yokomenuchi*, and vice versa, since it can be very difficult for tori to perceive which one of them uke will attack with. The same applies to *chudantsuki* and *jodantsuki*.

Jodantsuki is not necessary to include with the basics in tantodori, because it is an odd attack, but good to practice now and then. Tori should handle it the same way as *chudantsuki*.

The *tsuki* attack can be done with uke holding the tanto edge down, edge up, or edge to the side.

The *shomenuchi* attack is usually done with the same grip on the tanto as in *tsuki*, but in *yokomenuchi* the grip is reversed. Either grip can be used for both attack forms.

Ushiro chudantsuki is not exactly basic, but should be tried. It is most meaningful in *gotai*, from a static starting point, with uke already up close from behind, doing tsuki only upon tori's movement.

Certainly, tantodori can be practiced in *suwariwaza* and *hanmi handachiwaza*, but that is not to be regarded as basic. Anyway, the solutions are quite the same as for *tachiwaza*.

Notes on the techniques

IKKYO should be done with great care, so as not to get one's wrist or hand cut by the knife. Therefore, the *gokyo* style grab of uke's wrist is often the most trustworthy – but it is also possible to do ikkyo with the forearm meeting, like in unarmed shomenuchi and other strikes. If the attacking arm is low, as in chudantsuki, the gokyo grip is the most practical.

NIKYO in tantodori must be done with tori's arms extended, instead of pressing uke's hand to tori's shoulder, for obvious safety reasons. Also, the regular nikyo pinning at the end of the technique is questionable. It is better to do an *ikkyo* pinning, or a standing *kotegaeshi* pinning, to disarm uke. See also the comments on ikkyo above.

SANKYO in tantodori can be done disarming the uke already at the sankyo twisting of uke's wrist. The sankyo end pinning is not equally safe for disarming. The *gokyo* style grip on uke's wrist (as explained in the comments on *ikkyo* above) is not functional when doing sankyo, which has to start with a forearm meeting.

YONKYO is not really recommendable in tantodori, for safety reasons. It can be done, but it is not easy. The yonkyo grip is difficult to apply when uke holds a tanto, and the disarming in awkward. This should be kept in mind when the technique is practiced.

GOKYO is the most basic pinning technique in tantodori, because it is pretty much designed for that purpose, all the way to the end pinning and disarming.

HIJIKIME OSAE is not recommendable in tantodori, for safety reasons. It involves holding uke's knife hand close to tori's neck and chest. But the technique can be modified for increased safety. Some aikido teachers use it with confidence.

KAITEN OSAE is not recommendable in tantodori, for safety reasons. It involves uke's knife hand moving close to tori's face, neck and chest.

KOKYUHO in tantodori should be done so that it ends with disarming uke. Mostly, a *kotegaeshi* style ending works the best. Since it is a little tricky to get good control of uke's tanto hand in kokyuho, it should be regarded as advanced.

KOKYUNAGE in tantodori should be done so that it ends with disarming uke. This means holding on to uke through the throw. Mostly, a *kotegaeshi* style ending works the best.

IRIMINAGE in tantodori should be done so that it ends with disarming uke. This means keeping contact with uke through the throw. Mostly, a *kotegaeshi* style ending works the best.

SHIHONAGE in tantodori should be done so that it includes disarming uke. This can be done right before the throw, or immediately after it.

KOTEGAESHI is usually regarded as the easiest and most practical throwing technique in tantodori. It leads to a pinning, where tori is standing, and can disarm uke in an uncomplicated way.

TENCHINAGE in tantodori should be done so that it ends with disarming uke. This means holding on to uke through the throw. A *kotegaeshi* style ending works the best.

KAITENNAGE is not very practical at all in tantodori, since it does not lead to a pinning where uke can be disarmed. Therefore, it should not be included in the basics.

KOSHINAGE in tantodori should be done so that it ends with disarming uke. This means holding on to uke through the throw. Mostly, a *kotegaeshi* style ending works the best.

UDEKIMENAGE in tantodori should be done so that it ends with disarming uke. This means holding on to uke through the throw. A *kotegaeshi* style ending works the best.

JUJIGARAMI (also called JUJINAGE) does not really apply to tantodori, since it is difficult to safely get that control of both uke's arms.

USHIRO KIRIOTOSHI is not practical in tantodori, since it lacks the control of uke's knife arm.

AIKINAGE should not be applied to tantodori, for safety reasons. Also, it completely lacks the control of uke's knife arm.

AIKI OTOSHI does not apply to tantodori, because of how uke attacks, and because of the lack of control of uke's knife arm.

Tachidori　太刀取

Defense against sword

General notes
Techniques in parenthesis are less important or can be excluded in tachidori, because they are awkward to execute.

Crossed-out techniques should be excluded from tachidori, because they are unsuitable or impossible, or lack control of *tachi*, the sword.

Do not underestimate the difficulties in applying a technique and unarming uke, whose two-handed grip on the sword should be quite firm and solid.

bas = basic　adv = advanced/difficult　- = not basic/possible

TACHIDORI	shomen uchi	yokomen uchi	chudan tsuki	kesa giri	do	ushiro shomen uchi
KATAMEWAZA (pinning) *in order of importance*						
ikkyo omote/ura	bas	bas	bas	bas	bas	adv
~~nikyo omote/ura~~	-	-	-	-	-	-
(sankyo) omote/ura	adv	adv	adv	adv	adv	adv
~~yonkyo omote/ura~~	-	-	-	-	-	-
(gokyo) omote/ura	adv	adv	adv	adv	adv	adv
(hijikime osae) omote/ura	adv	adv	adv	adv	adv	adv
~~kaiten-osae omote/ura~~	-	-	-	-	-	-
NAGEWAZA (throw) *in order of importance*						
kokyuho	bas	adv	bas	adv	adv	adv
kokyunage	bas	bas	bas	bas	bas	adv
iriminage omote/ura	bas	bas	bas	bas	bas	adv
shihonage omote/ura	bas	bas	bas	bas	bas	adv
kotegaeshi omote/ura	bas	bas	bas	bas	bas	adv
~~tenchinage omote/ura~~	-	-	-	-	-	-
~~kaitennage omote/ura~~	-	-	-	-	-	-
koshinage	bas	bas	adv	adv	adv	adv
udekimenage	adv	adv	adv	adv	adv	adv
~~jujigarami~~	-	-	bas	bas	bas	-
~~(ushiro-kiriotoshi)~~	bas	bas	bas	bas	-	adv
~~aikinage~~	-	-	-	-	-	-
~~kiki-otoshi~~	-	-	-	-	-	-

Tachidori should always be done with good control of the sword, and end with disarming.

Returning the sword to uke should be done with care.

Notes on the attacks
Tori's entrance on *shomenuchi* should also protect against *yokomenuchi*, and vice versa, since it can be very difficult for tori to perceive which one of them uke will attack with. The same applies to *chudantsuki* and *jodantsuki*.

Jodantsuki is not necessary to include in the basics of tachidori, because of its similarity to *chudantsuki*, but good to practice now and then. Tori should handle it the same way as chudantsuki.

In *tsuki*, the sword is normally held with its edge down. It should also be tried with the edge up or to the side, but that is not basic.

Kesagiri, the diagonal cut, is rarely practiced, although it was the most common cut in traditional Japanese sword arts. For clarity in training, uke can start from *hasso*, the shoulder guard.

Do, or *yokogiri*, the sideway cut, is rarely practiced, but should be tried.

Ushiro shomenuchi is rarely practiced, and not basic. Anyway, it's good to try – carefully.

Tachidori can be practiced in *suwariwaza* and especially in *hanmi handachiwaza*, but that is not to be regarded as basic. Anyway, the solutions are quite the same as for *tachiwaza*.

Notes on the techniques
IKKYO can be done with the *gokyo* style grab of uke's wrist, but it is also possible to do ikkyo with the forearm meeting, like in unarmed shomenuchi and other attacks. If the attack

is low, as in chudantsuki, the gokyo grip is the most practical, and if high, the regular ikkyo style grip is easier.

NIKYO is very impractical in tachidori, since the sword is in the way. Also, uke's two-handed grip of the sword makes nikyo difficult to apply.

SANKYO is possible to do in tachidori, but quite complicated and difficult. Furthermore, it is hard to do with a trustworthy control of the sword. Still, it should be tried. Disarming uke should be done already at the sankyo twisting of uke's wrist. The sankyo end pinning is not practical for disarming. The *gokyo* style grip on uke's wrist (as explained in the comments on *ikkyo* above) is not functional when doing sankyo, which has to start with the forearm meeting.

YONKYO should be avoided in tachidori, since the sword is not at all controlled, so it easily gets in the way. Also, yonkyo is difficult to apply with any effect, when uke has a firm two-handed grip on the sword.

GOKYO usually differs distinctly from *ikkyo* only in the pinning at the end, and this pinning is mainly for *tantodori*. It is not that practical in tachidori, although possible.

HIJIKIME OSAE is not recommendable in tachidori, for safety reasons, since it involves leading uke's sword near tori's chest and face. But the technique can be modified for increased safety. Some aikido teachers do it with confidence.

KAITEN OSAE is not recommendable in tachidori, for safety reasons, since it involves uke's sword moving close to tori's face, neck and chest. It is also extremely difficult to do, because of uke's two-handed grip of the sword.

KOKYUHO in tachidori should be done so that it ends with disarming uke. Mostly, a *kotegaeshi* style ending works the best. It is easier to do kokyuho when moving to uke's right side (if uke grips the sword with the right hand in front of the left), than when moving to uke's left side.

KOKYUNAGE in tachidori should be done so that it ends

Taisabaki evasion in tachidori, defense against a sword attack, in this case jodantsuki. Seminar in Pardubice, Czech Republic. Photo by Leos Matousek.

with disarming uke. This means holding on to uke – or more often to *tsuka*, the hilt – through the throw. Mostly, a *kotegaeshi* style pinning works the best, if uke still holds on to the sword at the end of the throw.

IRIMINAGE in tachidori should be done so that it ends with disarming uke. This means keeping contact with uke through the throw. Mostly, a *kotegaeshi* style ending works the best. Some aikidoists disarm uke earlier in the technique, but that is less reliable, because it is usually done with just one hand, and therefore quite weak.

SHIHONAGE in tachidori should be done so that it includes disarming uke. This can be done right before the throw, or immediately after it – but most reliably the latter.

KOTEGAESHI is usually regarded as the easiest and most practical throwing technique in tachidori. It leads to a pinning where tori is standing and can disarm uke in an uncomplicated way. Still, if uke keeps a firm two-handed grip on the sword, both the throw and the disarming can become difficult.

TENCHINAGE is not practical in tachidori, because of uke's two-handed grip of the sword.

KAITENNAGE is not at all practical in tachidori, because of uke's two-handed grip of the sword. Also, it does not lead to a pinning where uke can be disarmed.

KOSHINAGE in tachidori should be done so that it ends with disarming uke. This means holding on to uke – or more often to *tsuka*, the hilt – through the throw. Mostly, a *kotegaeshi* style ending works the best. On attacks where uke ends at *chudankamae*, the middle level position, the technique is tricky to do, since tori has to get uke's arms up high.

UDEKIMENAGE in tachidori should be done so that it ends with disarming uke. This means holding on to uke through the throw, which is not easy due to uke's two-handed grip of the sword. A *kotegaeshi* style ending works the best.

Aikiken, sword against sword, at a seminar in Plzen, Czech Republic. Photo by Antonín Knízek.

JUJIGARAMI (also called JUJINAGE) does not really apply to tachidori, because of uke's two-handed grip of the sword – and the difficulty in doing the technique with control of the sword.

USHIRO KIRIOTOSHI is not practical in tachidori, since it lacks control of the sword. Except for that drawback, it can be done and should be tried.

AIKINAGE should not be applied to tachidori, for safety reasons. Also, it completely lacks control of the sword, and a possibility to disarm uke.

AIKI OTOSHI does not apply to tachidori, because of how uke attacks. Also, it lacks control of the sword.

Jodori

Defense against staff

General notes

Crossed-out techniques should be excluded from jodori, because they are unsuitable or very difficult, or lack control of the jo.

Most jodori techniques can be done either on the arm uke extends in the attack, or on the arm uke holds back. Usually, the former is more basic and easy, but that depends on what side of uke tori enters. A solution similar to that of *tachidori* is to be regarded as the most basic, when this can be decided.

Do not underestimate the difficulty in applying a technique and unarming uke, whose two-handed grip of the jo can be quite firm and solid.

JODORI	choku tsuki	kaeshi tsuki	yokomen uchi	gedan uchi
KATAMEWAZA (pinning) *in order of importance*				
ikkyo omote/ura	bas	bas	bas	bas
nikyo omote/ura	bas	bas	bas	bas
sankyo omote/ura	bas	bas	bas	bas
yonkyo omote/ura	adv	adv	adv	adv
gokyo omote/ura	-	-	-	-
hijikime osae omote/ura	bas	bas	bas	bas
~~kaiten osae omote/ura~~	-	-	-	-
NAGEWAZA (throw) *in order of importance*				
kokyuho	bas	bas	bas	bas
kokyunage	bas	bas	bas	bas
iriminage omote/ura	bas	bas	bas	bas
shihonage omote/ura	bas	bas	bas	bas
kotegaeshi omote/ura	adv	adv	adv	adv
~~tenchinage omote/ura~~	-	-	-	-
~~kaitennage omote/ura~~	-	-	-	-
koshinage	bas	bas	bas	bas
udekimenage	adv	adv	-	-
jujigarami	-	-	-	-
ushiro kiriotoshi	-	-	-	-
aikinage	-	-	-	-
aiki otoshi	-	-	-	-

bas = basic
adv = advanced/difficult
- = not basic/possible

Jodori should always be done with good control of the jo, and end with disarming. The disarming is often quite complicated, because of tori's two-handed grip of the jo.

Returning the jo to uke should be done with care.

Notes on the attacks
Observe the differences for tori when uke holds *choku*, with the front hand on the jo straight like in a sword grip, or *kaeshi*, with the front hand on the jo reversed.

Kaeshitsuki is sometimes called *gyakutsuki*.

Techniques on *yokomenuchi* and *gedanuchi* are either done like on *chokutsuki* or like on *kaeshitsuki*, depending on uke's grip of the jo.

Basic techniques on *jodantsuki*, to the head or neck, and on *gedantsuki*, to the knee, are done like on *chudantsuki*.

Gedanuchi with the jo is a swing strike to the knee. It is rarely trained in aikido jodori, but should be tried.

Shomenuchi with the jo is an impractical attack, and therefore excluded.

Kote, wrist strike, with the jo is only meaningful against an armed opponent, and therefore excluded from jodori.

Jodori can be practiced in *suwariwaza* and especially in *hanmi handachiwaza*, but that is not to be regarded as basic. Anyway, the solutions are much the same as for *tachiwaza*.

All attacks in jodori can be done with the right arm in front of the left, or vice versa.

Notes on the techniques
IKKYO is easy enough on all attacks, and on uke's outer as well as inner arm. The disarming of uke, though, can be tricky.

NIKYO is easier to do on uke's inner arm, because of the two-handed grip.

SANKYO is easier to do on uke's inner arm, because of the two-handed grip.

YONKYO is not practical in jodori, because of the lack of control of tori's jo. It needs to be done on the inner arm.

GOKYO is just like *ikkyo* on uke's outer arm, but it cannot end with the typical gokyo pinning, so there is no reason to include it among the basics.

HIJIKIME OSAE can be done on all jodori attacks, and is quite practical at that. It is slightly easier to do on uke's outer arm.

KAITEN OSAE is just not possible in jodori, because of uke's two-handed grip on the jo. So, it is excluded.

KOKYUHO is quite easy to do on all jodori attack forms, particularly on the side of uke's outer arm.

KOKYUNAGE is easy to do on all jodori attack forms, and on both sides of uke.

IRIMINAGE is easy to do on the side of uke's outer arm, but significantly more difficult on the other side of uke – especially when it comes to controlling the jo.

SHIHONAGE can be done rather easily on both sides of uke. The side of uke's outer arm is most common, although the inner arm side is more practical.

KOTEGAESHI is possible to do on all the jodori attack forms, but difficult because of uke's grips on the jo, stabilizing uke's hands. The technique should be done on uke's outer arm.

TENCHINAGE is not practical in jodori, since it is not possible to extend uke's arms in the way needed.

KAITENNAGE is not possible in jodori, because of uke's two-handed grip on the jo.

Morihiro Saito, 9 dan Aikikai, and Ulf Evenås, 7 dan Aikikai, in a jo against jo exercise at Iwama, Japan. Photo by Jöran Fagerlund.

KOSHINAGE is quite easy to do in jodori, on both sides of uke. It is the easiest on the side of uke's inner arm.

UDEKIMENAGE is possible, although difficult, on jo *tsuki* attacks, but should be avoided on the *uchi* attacks, because the technique needs an entrance to the side of uke's outer arm.

JUJIGARAMI (also called JUJINAGE) is not possible in jodori, because of uke's two-handed grip on the jo, and is therefore excluded.

USHIRO KIRIOTOSHI is possible to do on jodori attacks, but it lacks control of the jo and will not lead to the necessary disarming, so it is excluded.

AIKINAGE should not be applied to jodori, for safety reasons. Also, it completely lacks control of the jo, and a possibility to disarm uke.

AIKI OTOSHI does not apply to jodori, because of how uke attacks. Also, it lacks control of the jo.

Kaeshiwaza 返技

Counter techniques

KAESHIWAZA uke's technique horizontal tori's kaeshiwaza vertical	ikkyo	nikyo	san kyo	irimi nage	shiho nage	kote gaeshi	tenchi nage	ude kime nage	kokyu ho	koshi nage	kaiten nage
KATAMEWAZA (pinning) *in order of importance*			*bas = basic*		*adv = advanced/difficult*			*- =not basic/possible*			
ikkyo omote/ura	bas	bas	bas	bas	bas	adv	-	bas	bas	bas	adv
nikyo omote/ura	bas	-	-	bas	bas	bas	-	adv	bas	-	adv
sankyo omote/ura	bas	bas	bas	-	-	-	bas	-	-	-	adv
yonkyo omote/ura	-	-	bas	-	-	-	bas	-	-	-	adv
(gokyo) omote/ura	-	-	-	-	-	-	-	-	-	-	-
(hijikime osae) omote/ura	-	-	-	-	-	-	-	-	-	-	-
(kaiten osae) omote/ura	-	-	-	-	-	-	-	-	-	-	-
NAGEWAZA (throw) *in order of importance*			*bas = basic*		*adv = advanced/difficult*			*- =not basic/possible*			
kokyuho	bas	-	-	-	bas	bas	adv	bas	bas	-	adv
kokyunage	bas	bas	bas	-	bas	bas	-	bas	bas	bas	adv
iriminage omote/ura	bas	bas	bas	bas	bas	bas	adv	adv	bas	adv	adv
shihonage omote/ura	bas	adv	-	-	bas	adv	bas	bas	bas	adv	adv
kotegaeshi omote/ura	bas	adv	-	-	adv	-	-	bas	bas	adv	adv
tenchinage omote/ura	-	-	-	-	-	-	bas	-	bas	-	adv
kaitennage omote/ura	-	-	-	adv	-	adv	adv	-	-	-	adv
koshinage	bas	bas	-	-	adv	-	-	bas	-	bas	adv
udekimenage	bas	adv	-	-	bas	bas	-	bas	adv	adv	adv
(jujigarami)	-	-	-	-	-	-	-	-	-	-	-
ushiro-kiriotoshi	-	-	-	-	-	-	-	-	-	-	-
aikinage	-	-	-	-	-	-	-	-	-	-	-
aiki-otoshi	-	-	-	-	-	-	-	-	-	-	-

General notes

Techniques in parenthesis are less important or can be excluded in kaeshiwaza, because they are awkward to execute.

Crossed-out techniques should be excluded from kaeshiwaza, because the situation does not open for them.

A correctly done technique on a sincere attack should not really be possible to counter with kaeshiwaza.

Countering is done by "switching roles" from uke to tori, at a certain point, by treating the partner's aikido technique as an attack.

In basic techniques, the "switching of roles" should happen at a moment when the initial aikido technique has become specific, i.e. recognizable as that certain aikido technique.

Because kaeshiwaza starts well into the technique, it hardly matters what the initial attack form was.

Kaeshiwaza should be seen as a way of improving the aikido techniques, so that they become increasingly difficult to counter.

Notes on the techniques

IKKYO should not be countered before uke's arm is lifted in an arch. It is relatively easy to counter with most techniques, except tenchinage, because of the partner's arm positions.

NIKYO should not be countered before uke's hand is positioned for the nikyo wrist twist. Because of this position, several techniques are impractical against it.

SANKYO should not be countered before uke's hand is positioned for the sankyo wrist twist. Because of this position, several techniques are impractical against it.

YONKYO should not be countered before uke's arm is positioned for the yonkyo pressure. Because of tori's two-handed grip, most techniques are impractical against it.

GOKYO is not practical to counter, since it doesn't really become gokyo before the end pinning, and that is too late for kaeshiwaza.

HIJIKIME OSAE can be countered, but it is quite risky because of the elbow lock. It should be avoided, or practiced with care. Solutions are difficult on most counter techniques, because of tori's arm positions.

KAITEN OSAE is not that meaningful in kaeshiwaza, since it has to be countered before it clearly has become kaiten osae.

KOKYUHO can be countered at tori's first move, but not after tori has started the actual throw. It is reasonably easy to counter with most techniques.

KOKYUNAGE can be countered when the actual throw commences, but preferably right before that. It is rather easy to counter with most techniques.

IRIMINAGE should not be countered before tori moves the throwing arm toward uke. It can be countered with most techniques.

SHIHONAGE should not be countered before uke's arm has been lifted. Most counter techniques can be used, although with differing difficulty.

KOTEGAESHI should not be countered before tori prepares to turn uke's wrist. Because of tori's hand positions, several counter techniques become impractical.

TENCHINAGE is difficult to counter, since it is quite late in the technique that it becomes recognizable as tenchinage, and few options remain.

KAITENNAGE is quite difficult to counter, since it is quite late in the technique that it becomes recognizable as kaiten-nage, and by then uke's position is weakened.

KOSHINAGE should not be countered before tori has as-

Kokyunage at the author's dojo Enighet, Sweden.

sumed a throwing position. Some counter techniques are quite easy, others very impractical.

UDEKIMENAGE should not be countered before tori has positioned uke's arm for the throw. Several counter techniques are quite easy, but some impractical.

JUJIGARAMI (also called JUJINAGE) is not practical to counter, since it is too late in the technique that it is recognizable as jujigarami, and by then uke's arms are locked.

USHIRO KIRIOTOSHI is not practical to counter, since it becomes recognizable right at the throwing moment.

AIKINAGE is not practical to counter, because it becomes recognizable at the very moment of the throw.

AIKI OTOSHI is not practical to counter, because it becomes recognizable too late in the technique, where uke's options are few.

Aikido

Henkawaza 変化技

Changed techniques

bas = basic   adv = advanced/difficult   - = not basic/possible

HENKAWAZA — initial technique horisontal / next technique vertical	ikkyo	nikyo	san kyo	kokyu ho	kokyu nage	irimi nage	shiho nage	kote gaeshi	tenchi nage	kaiten nage	koshi nage	ude kime nage
KATAMEWAZA (pinning) *in order of importance*												
ikkyo omote/ura	-	-	-	bas	bas	bas	-	-	bas	bas	bas	bas
nikyo omote/ura	-	-	-	-	bas	-	-	-	adv	-	-	-
sankyo omote/ura	-	bas	-	-	-	-	-	bas	-	-	bas	-
yonkyo omote/ura	-	-	-	-	-	-	-	adv	-	-	-	-
(gokyo) omote/ura	-	-	-	-	-	-	-	-	-	-	-	-
hijikime osae omote/ura	-	-	-	-	-	-	-	-	-	adv	-	-
kaiten osae omote/ura	-	adv	-	-	-	-	-	-	adv	-	-	-
NAGEWAZA (throw) *in order of importance*												
kokyuho	bas	-	bas	-	bas	bas	bas	bas	bas	bas	adv	bas
kokyunage	bas	bas	bas	bas	-	-	-	bas	bas	bas	bas	adv
iriminage omote/ura	bas	bas	adv	bas	bas	-	bas	bas	-	-	bas	bas
shihonage omote/ura	bas	-	adv	adv	bas	-	-	bas	bas	-	adv	bas
kotegaeshi omote/ura	bas	-	adv	adv	adv	-	bas	bas	-	-	adv	-
tenchinage omote/ura	-	-	-	adv	adv	-	-	-	-	-	adv	-
kaitennage omote/ura	-	adv	adv	-	-	-	bas	-	bas	-	-	-
koshinage	-	bas	bas	adv	-	bas	bas	-	-	-	-	bas
udekimenage	bas	-	-	-	bas	bas	bas	-	adv	-	adv	-
(jujigarami)	-	-	-	-	-	adv	bas	-	-	-	-	adv
ushiro kiriotoshi	bas	bas	adv	-	-	adv	bas	bas	-	-	-	-
(aikinage)	-	-	-	-	-	-	-	-	-	-	adv	adv
aiki otoshi	-	-	-	-	-	-	-	-	-	-	adv	adv

General notes
Henkawaza in the meaning of variations on techniques should not be regulated as basics, but can still be required in grading.

Here, the henkawaza intended is the shifting from one technique to another.

Techniques in parenthesis are less important or can be excluded in henkawaza, because they are awkward to execute.

The shift of technique should be done when the initial technique has become specific, i.e. recognizable as a certain aikido technique.

Ikkyo is a general entrance to several techniques, so it is only included in henkawaza when followed by a technique that normally is done with a different entrance.

The shift of technique should be done smoothly.

Henkawaza should be a motivated shift, such as when meeting resistance in the initial technique, or when uke gets out of position for the initial technique, or at need in *taninzugake*, etc.

Henkawaza should not be trained so that it impairs the basic techniques (for example by doing a sloppy initial technique to motivate the shift).

Notes on the techniques
IKKYO in henkawaza is not changed into other pinnings, but techniques that don't normally start like ikkyo. It should not be changed before uke's arm is lifted in an arch.

NIKYO should not be changed before uke's hand is positioned for the nikyo wrist twist. Because of this position, several techniques are impractical.

SANKYO should not be changed before uke's hand is positioned for the sankyo wrist twist. Because of this position, several techniques are impractical.

Aikido

YONKYO should not be changed before uke's arm is positioned for the yonkyo pressure. Because of tori's two-handed grip, most techniques are awkward and impractical to change into.

GOKYO is not practical to change, since it doesn't really become gokyo before the end pinning.

HIJIKIME OSAE can be changed, but it is odd and awkward because of tori's and uke's positions when hijikime osae is recognizable as such. Because of uke's position, only kaitennage makes good sense.

KAITEN OSAE is possible but difficult to change to a few techniques, and very impractical to the rest, because of uke's position when the kaiten osae is recognizable.

KOKYUHO can be changed into most techniques with ease. It should not be done before tori has moved into the throwing position.

KOKYUNAGE can be changed to many techniques. It should not be done before tori has commenced the throw. There, it is quite practical to have as an option, if uke resists the throw.

IRIMINAGE should not be changed before tori has entered the throwing position. It is easy to change into several other techniques, most of them quite practical if uke resists.

SHIHONAGE should not be changed before uke's arm has been lifted. Most techniques can be used, although with differing difficulty.

KOTEGAESHI should not be changed before tori prepares to turn uke's wrist. Because of tori's hand positions, several techniques become impractical.

TENCHINAGE is difficult and impractical to change, since it is quite late in the technique that it becomes recognizable as tenchinage, where few options remain.

KAITENNAGE is quite difficult and impractical to change,

since it is quite late in the technique that it becomes recognizable as kaitennage, where few options remain.

KOSHINAGE should not be changed before tori has assumed a throwing position, and maybe even tried the throw. Some techniques are quite easy, and very practical to have as options if uke resists the throw.

UDEKIMENAGE should not be changed before tori has positioned uke's arm for the throw. Several techniques are quite easy, but some impractical.

JUJIGARAMI (also called JUJINAGE) is not practical to change, since it is too late into the technique that it is recognizable as jujigarami.

USHIRO KIRIOTOSHI is easy to change at the moment it becomes recognizable, because the break of balance smoothly leads to some techniques. Other techniques, though, are quite impractical.

AIKINAGE is not practical to change, because it becomes recognizable at the very moment of the throw.

AIKI OTOSHI is not practical to change, because it becomes recognizable too late in the technique, where tori's options are few.

Renzokuwaza 連続技

Consecutive techniques

General notes
Renzokuwaza is the practice where tori makes several techniques consecutively, without uke making new attacks in between.

Each technique is completed, except for an end pinning, and the next one commences as soon as uke stands up.

This is an exercise of improvisation and continued flow. Because of this, there is not much point in systematizing renzokuwaza. That is why no table is included for it, nor any specific comments on the aikido techniques.

Since it becomes renzokuwaza long after the initial attack, and no new proper attacks are allowed within a set of consecutive techniques, comments on the attack forms are also irrelevant.

A set of renzokuwaza techniques is usually ended with a pinning, or with a throw that distances uke from tori.

Renzokuwaza is practiced in *jutai* or *kinagare*, in movement, but not in *gotai*, from static positions.

Primarily, renzokuwaza is a way of exercising a relaxed and continued flow. It is also an exercise in proper timing. For uke, it is important to hurry standing up after each technique, which is the natural tendency of any attacker.

Aikido

Glossary of aikido terms

A

ai harmony, unity, blending

aihanmi basic relation between partners: both have same foot forward (left or right), compare *gyakuhanmi*

aihanmi katatedori wrist grip, right on right or left on left, also called *kosadori*, compare *gyakuhanmi katatedori*

aiki blending/uniting one's ki with that of the partner

aikibatto sword exercises, solo or pair

aikibudo budo based on the aiki principle, earlier name for aikido

aikido the way through the life energy to harmony/unity

aikidoka one who does aikido, specifically on an advanced or professional level

aikido toho Nishio sensei's iaido school

Aikijinja the aikido temple in Iwama

aikijo aikido jo-staff exercises

aikijutsu name on the Daito ryu martial art, also called *aiki-jujutsu*

Aikikai organization and "label" for Morihei Ueshiba's aikido

aikiken aikido sword exercises

aikinage aiki-throw, throwing technique

aiki no michi aikido (michi=do)

aikiotoshi aiki-drop, throwing technique

aikitaiso aikido warm-up exercises

aite partner in training

arigato thanks

arigato gozaimasu thanks for something going on

arigato gozaimashita thanks for something completed

ashi leg, foot

ate hit, strike

atemi strike to the body

awase harmonizing/blending movement

ayumiashi altering steps, left and right, like normal walking, compare *tsugiashi*

B

barai/harai parry, ward off
batto draw the sword, also called *nuki*
bo staff, longer than the *jo*
bokken wooden training sword
bokuto same as *bokken*
bu war, battle, fight
budo the way of war/battle, the Japanese martial arts
budoka one who does any budo, specifically on an advanced or professional level
bugei battle art, old term
bukiwaza weapons training
bushi warrior
bushido the way of the warrior

C

chado tea ceremony
chikara force/strength
choku direct
chokutsuki direct strike with the *jo*
chudan middle, compare *jodan* and *gedan*
chudankamae guard position with a weapon at belly height
chudantsuki strike at belly/solar plexus, with weapon or empty hand
chukyusha continuing student, with a mid-level kyu grade, compare *jokyusha*

D

dai big, also o
daisho sword pair, the long and the short sword
Daito ryu *aikijutsu* school
dame wrong, bad
dan level, black belt grade in budo
dao/tao transcription of the Chinese word for way, *do*
deshi student
do way, also *michi*
dogi training dress, also *keikogi*
do-in self massage tradition

dojo training hall
dojo cho head of a training hall
doka poem about the way
domo much
domo arigato gozaimasu thank you so much, for something going on
domo arigato gozaimashita thank you so much, for something completed
dori take, catch, grab
dosa movement
doshu way leader, head of a budo art
dozo please/by all means

E
embukai public demonstration
empi strike with elbow
eri neck, collar
eridori collar grip by the neck

F
fukushidoin assisting instructor, title for aikido teacher, 2-3 dan, compare *shidoin* and *shihan*
funakogi undo, rowing exercise, also called *torifune*
furitama exercise to still ki
futaridori/futarigake two attackers

G
gaeshi/kaeshi returning, reversed
gamae/kamae guard, basic position
gasshuku training camp, lodging together
gedan low, compare *jodan* and *chudan*
gedanbarai low block
geiko/keiko training
geri kick
gi dress, as in *dogi* or *keikogi*
giri/kiri cut
go five
gokyo fifth teaching, pinning technique

gomen nasai excuse me
Gorin no sho *Book of Five Rings,* book written by Miyamoto Musashi in the 17th century
gotai/kotai hard body, static training, compare *jutai, ryutai,* and *kinagare*
gyaku reverse, opposite
gyakuhanmi basic relation between partners: they have opposite foot forward, compare *aihanmi*
gyakuhanmi katatedori wrist grip, right on left or left on right, compare *aihanmi katatedori*
gyakutsuki strike with opposing arm and leg forward, compare *oitsuki*

H
hachi eight
Hagakure *Hiding the Leaves,* classic samurai book from the 18th century
hai yes
hajime begin
hakama traditional wide pants, used in aikido
handachi half standing
hanmi half body
hanmigamae angled guard position
hanmi handachiwaza sitting versus standing
hanshi title in kendo, from 8th dan, compare *renshi* and *kyushi*
hantai opposed
happo eight directions, compare *shiho*
hara stomach
harai/barai sweep away, parry
harakiri cut belly, ritual suicide, also called *seppuku*
hassogaeshi *jo* staff technique
hassogamae guard with weapon at shoulder level
henkawaza, changing techniques, variations on basic techniques, also shifting from one technique to another
hidari left (right: *migi*)
hiji elbow
hijidori grip on elbow

hijikimeosae pinning technique, sometimes called *rokkyo*
hiki pull
hineri twist
hiragana Japanese phonetic writing, compare *katakana*
hito e mi making the body small, guard position with more of an angle than *hanmi*
hiza knee
ho method
ho direction, side
hombu head quarters
Hombu dojo head dojo, used for the Aikikai head dojo in Tokyo

I
iaido the art of drawing the Japanese sword
iaito training sword, usually not sharpened
ichi one
ichiban first, best
iie no
iki willpower
ikkajo older term for *ikkyo*
ikki one *ki*, bottoms up, toast
ikkyo first teaching, pinning technique
ikkyo undo exercise of the basic *ikkyo* movement
in Japanese for the Chinese concept *yin*, compare *yo*
ippon one point
ipponken strike with one knuckle
irimi in to the body, inward, compare *tenkan*
iriminage inward throw, throwing technique
Iwama Japanese town, where Osensei had a dojo and a home
Iwama ryu Saito sensei's aikido style

J
jiyuwaza free training
jo wooden staff, 127.5 centimeters
jo awase *jo* staff exercises
jodan high, compare *chudan* and *gedan*

jodankamae guard with weapon over head

jodantsuki strike at head

jodanuke high block

jodo the way of the staff

jodori defense against *jo* staff

jokyusha advanced student, with a higher kyu grade, compare *chukyusha*

ju ten

ju soft

judo the soft way, or the way to softness

jujigarami/jujinage cross throw

jujutsu the soft art

jumbitaiso warm-up exercises, also called *aikitaiso*

juntsuki strike with the same arm and leg forward, also called *oitsuki*, compare *gyakutsuki*

jutai soft body, smooth training, compare *gotai*, *ryutai*, and *kinagare*

jutsu technique or art

K

kaeshi/gaeshi returning, reverse

kaeshitsuki reverse strike with *jo* staff

kaeshiwaza counter techniques

kagamibiraki Japanese New Year celebration, held January 11

kai club, association

kaiso founder

kaitennage rotation throw, throwing technique

kaitenosae rotation pinning technique

kakaedori embrace

kakarigeiko attackers in line, one after the other

kakudo angle

kamae/gamae guard position

kami divinity

kamiza honorary place in a dojo, compare *shomen* and *shinzen*

kampai cheers, toast

kan intuition

kangeiko mid-winter training

kanji ideograms, the Chinese writing

kanren linked, connected

kanrenwaza linked techniques, one technique followed by another, compare *renzokuwaza*

kansetsu joint on body

karatedo the way of the empty hand, or the way through the hand to emptiness

Kashima shintoryu traditional sword school

kata form, pre-decided movements

kata shoulder

katadori shoulder grip

katadori menuchi shoulder grip followed by *shomenuchi*

katakana Japanese phonetic writing, compare *hiragana*

katamewaza pinning techniques

katana the Japanese sword, also *ken, to,* and *tachi*

katate one-handed technique

katatedori wrist grip

katate ryotedori grip with both hands, also called *morotedori*

Katori shintoryu traditional sword school

keiko/geiko training

keikogi training dress, also *dogi*

ken sword, also *katana, to,* and *tachi*

kendo Japanese fencing

ki spirit, life energy

kiai gathered *ki*, usually used for shout in budo

ki-aikido Tohei sensei's aikido style

kihon basics

kihonwaza basic training

kikai tanden the ocean of *ki* in the body's center

kime focusing

kimusubi tying one's *ki* to that of the partner

kinagare/ki no nagare streaming ki, flowing training, compare *gotai, jutai,* and *ryutai*

Ki no kenkyukai Tohei sensei's aikido school, also *Shinshin toitsu*

kiri/giri cut

kirikaeshi turning cut, sword exercise

koan riddle in *Zen*
kobudo older budo
kogeki attack
kogekiho attack techniques
kohai one's junior, compare *sempai*
Kojiki religious Japanese book from the 8th century
kokoro heart, will, mind, also pronounced *shin*
kokyu breathing
kokyuho breathing exercise, throwing technique
kokyunage breath throw
kokyu ryoku breath power
kosa cross over, pass
kosadori cross-over grip, same as *aihanmi katatedori*
koshi hip
koshinage hip throw
kotai see *gotai*
kote wrist
kotegaeshi reversed wrist, throwing technique
kotehineri twisted wrist, *sankyo*
kotemawashi turned wrist, *nikyo*
kotodama/kototama spirit of words, Japanese cosmology based on sounds
ku nine
ku emptiness
kubi neck
kubishime neck choke
kuden oral tradition or teaching
kumi group, set
kumijo *jo* staff exercises, jo against jo
kumitachi sword exercises, sword against sword
kumite empty handed fight
kumiuchi ancient Japanese wrestling in full armor
kuzushi break balance
kyo principle, learning
kyoshi title in kendo, 6-7 dan, compare *renshi* and *hanshi*
kyu grade before blackbelt, compare *dan*
kyudo the way of the bow and arrow

L
(L not used in Japanese)

M
ma distance between training partners
maai harmonious, balanced distance between training partners
mae front, forward, compare *ushiro*
maegeri straight kick
mae ukemi forward fall, compare *ushiro ukemi*
makiwara target for hitting practice in karatedo
maru circle
mawashi revolving, turning
mawashigeri roundhouse kick
mawate turning
me eye
men head
michi way, also *do*
migi right (left: *hidari*)
misogi purification, cleansing
mochi hold or grip, also called *dori*
mochikata gripping attacks
mo ikkai do again
mokuso meditation, also called *zazen*
moro both
morotedori grip with both hands, also called *katate ryotedori*
mu nothing, empty
mushin empty mind
mudansha trainee without dan grade, compare *yudansha*
mune chest
munedori collar grip by the chest
musubi tie together

N
nagare flow, streaming
nage throw, also used for the one doing the aikido technique, compare *tori*
nagewaza throwing techniques

naginata Japanese halberd
nakaima here and now
nana seven, also pronounced *shichi*
nen the purity and unity of the mind
ni two
Nihon/Nippon Japan
Nihongi religious Japanese book from the 8th century
nikajo older name for *nikyo*
nikyo second teaching, pinning technique
nin person
ninindori two attackers, also called *futaridori*
ninja courier and spy in old Japan
Nippon/Nihon Japan
Nito ichiryu/Niten ichiryu School of Two Swords/Two Heavens, Miyamoto Musashi's sword school
noto return the sword to the scabbard
nuki draw the sword, also called *batto*
nukite strike with fingertips

O
o big, also *dai*
obi belt
ocha tea
oitsuki strike with same arm and foot forward, also called *jontsuki*
omote front, surface, compare *ura*
Omotokyo a Shinto society
onegai shimasu please, asking for something
osae press down, pinning
osensei great teacher, in aikido Morihei Ueshiba
otagai ni rei bow to each others
otoshi drop
oyowaza applied techniques, modified for efficiency

P
(P rarely used in Japanese)

Q
(Q not used in Japanese)

R
randori disorderly grabbing, free training
rei bow
reigi etiquette, also called *reishiki*
renshi title in kendo, 4-6 dan, compare *hanshi* and *kyoshi*
renshu training
renzoku continuous
renzoku uchikomi *jo* staff exercise
renzokuwaza consecutive techniques, a series of techniques
ritsurei standing bow
rokkyo sixth teaching, pinning technique, see *hijikime osae*
roku six
ryo both
ryotedori gripping both wrists
ryu school
ryutai flowing body, fluid training, compare *gotai, jutai,* and *kinagare*

S
sabaki action or handling
sake rice wine
samurai to serve, Japanese warrior class
san three
sankajo older term for *sankyo*
sankaku triangle
sankakutai triangle shape, position of the feet in *hanmi*
sankyo third teaching, pinning technique
sannindori/sanningake three attackers
sanpo three directions
satori enlightenment in *Zen*
saya scabbard
seika no itten, the one point below the navel, the body center, also called *tanden*
seiki life energy
seiza correct sitting, sit on knees

sempai one's senior, compare *kohai*

sen no sen before the attack, countering before the strike

sensei teacher

sensen no sen before before the attack, a leading initiative

seppuku cut belly, ritual suicide with sword, also called *harakiri*

shi four, also pronounced *yon*

shiai competition

shiatsu massage

shichi seven, also pronounced *nana*

shidoin instructor, middle title for aikido teacher, 4-5 dan, compare *fukushidoin* and *shihan*

shihan expert example, high title for aikido teacher, from 6 dan, compare *fukushidoin* and *shidoin*

shiho four directions

shihonage four directions throw, throwing technique

shikaku square

shikaku dead angle

shiki courage

shikko knee walking

shime choke

shin heart, will, mind, also pronounced *kokoro*

shinai kendo sword of bamboo

Shindo Musoryu *jodo* school

shinken sharp authentic Japanese sword

Shinshin toitsu Tohei sensei's aikido school, *Ki no kenkyukai*

Shinto the way of the gods, Japanese religion

shinzen seat of the gods, in a dojo usually a position on the wall farthest from the entrance, compare *kamiza* and *shomen*

shisei posture

shite the one leading, defender in aikido, also called *tori* or *nage*

shizentai natural body posture

sho first, beginning

shodan first dan grade

shodo calligraphy

Shodokan Tomiki sensei's aikido school

shomen front of the head

Shoji Nishio, 8 dan Aikikai, shows an atemi entrance at a seminar in the author's dojo Enighet, Sweden. Photo by Ulf Lundquist.

shomen head place of the dojo, compare *shinzen* and *kamiza*
shomen ni rei bow to head place of the dojo
shomenuchi strike to head
shoshinsha beginner
shuto hand side strike
sode sleeve
sodedori sleeve grip
sodeguchidori grip on the cuff of the sleeve
soto outside, outer, compare *uchi*
sotodeshi student who lives outside the dojo, compare *uchi-deshi*
sotokaiten outer rotation, compare *uchikaiten*
sotouke block from outside, compare *uchiuke*
suburi basic exercises with sword or staff
suki opening
sumi corner
sumikiri sharpness of body and mind
sumimasen excuse me
sumo traditional Japanese wrestling

suri rub, scrape
sutemiwaza techniques with losing one's own balance
suwariwaza seated training, also called *suwate*
suwate seated training, also called *suwariwaza*

T
tachi sword, also *to, ken,* and *katana*
tachi standing
tachidori defense against sword
tachiwaza training standing up
tai body
taijutsu body techniques, unarmed techniques
tai no henko body turn, also called *tai no tenkan*
tai no tenkan body turn, also called *tai no henko*
taisabaki body move, evasive movement in aikido
taiso exercises
takemusu improvised martial art
takemusu aiki improvised martial art through the principle
of *aiki*
tambo short staff
tameshi test
tameshigiri cutting test with sword
tameshiware hitting test in karatedo
tanden body center, compare *seika no itten*
taninzugake several attackers
tanren drill
tanto/tanken knife
tantodori defense against knife
tao/dao Chinese for *do*
tatami mat
tate stand up
te hand
tegatana hand sword, hand in sword-like movements
tekubi wrist
tekubiosae pinned wrist, *yonkyo*
tenchinage heaven-earth throw, throwing technique
tenkan turn
tettsui hammer strike

to sword, also *ken, tachi,* and *katana*
tobigeri jump kick
tobikoshi fall over hip, break fall
tomauchi *jo* staff technique
tori the one who takes, defender in aikido, also called *nage* and *shite*
torifune rowing exercise, also called *funakogi undo*
tsuba sword guard
tsugiashi following step, back foot following and not passing front foot, compare *ayumiashi*
tsuka sword hilt
tsuki strike, with a weapon or empty hand

U
uchi hit
uchi inside, within, inner, compare *soto*
uchideshi student living in the dojo, compare *sotodeshi*
uchikaiten inner rotation, compare *sotokaiten*
uchikata striking and hitting attack forms
uchikomi hitting repeatedly
uchiuke block from inside, compare *sotouke*
ude arm
udekimenage arm lock throw
udenobashi extended arm, *gokyo*
udeosae pinned arm, *ikkyo*
uke the one receiving, attacker in aikido
uke block, parry
ukemi falling
undo exercise
ura backside, inside, reverse side, compare *omote*
uraken backhand strike
ushiro behind, backwards, compare *mae*
ushirogeri backward kick
ushiro kiriotoshi rear cutting drop, throwing technique
ushiro ukemi backward fall, compare *mae ukemi*
ushirowaza attacks from behind

Taninzugake evasion of multiple attackers with bokken, at a seminar in Plzen, Czech Republic. Photo by Antonín Knízek.

V

(V not used in Japanese)

W

waka sensei young teacher, used in aikido for the successor of *doshu*
waki side
wakizashi short sword
ware break, split
waza technique, skill, training method

X

(X not used in Japanese)

Y

yame stop
yang sunny side, male pole, in Japanese *yo*, compare *yin*
yari spear
yawara old *jujutsu*
yin shady side, female pole, in Japanese *in*, compare *yang*
yo Japanese for *yang*
yoko side, sideways, horizontal

yokogeri side kick
yokogiri side cut
yokomen side of the head
yokomenuchi strike to the side of the head
yoko ukemi side fall
yon four, also pronounced *shi*
yonkajo older term for *yonkyo*
yonkyo fourth teaching, pinning technique
Yoseikan Mochizuki sensei's aikido school
Yoshinkan Shioda sensei's aikido school
yudansha dan graded, compare *mudansha*

Z

za seated, sit
Zaidan Hojin Aikikai Aikikai Foundation
zanshin remaining spirit, continued concentration
zarei sitting bow
zazen sitting meditation, also called *mokuso*
Zen a form of buddhism
zengo around, forward and back, front and rear
zori sandals

Numbers

1   ichi
2   ni
3   san
4   shi / yon
5   go
6   roku
7   shichi / nana
8   hachi
9   ku
10   ju
20   ni-ju
21   ni-ju-ichi
100 hyaku
1000 sen

Lightning Source UK Ltd.
Milton Keynes UK
176214UK00002B/133/P